Fueling THE FUTURE

Oil

Other books in the Fueling the Future series:

Fueling THE FUTURE

Oil

Crystal McCage, *Book Editor*

Christine Nasso, *Publisher*
Elizabeth Des Chenes, *Managing Editor*

GREENHAVEN PRESS
An imprint of Thomson Gale, a part of The Thomson Corporation

Detroit • New York • San Francisco • New Haven, Conn. • Waterville, Maine • London

LIBRARY OF CONGRESS CATALOGING-IN-PUBLICATION DATA

Oil / Crystal McCage, book editor.
    p. cm. — (Fueling the future)
Includes bibliographical references and index.
ISBN 13: 978-0-7377-3588-8 (alk. paper)
ISBN 10: 0-7377-3588-0 (alk. paper)
1. Petroleum as fuel—History.   2. Petroleum as fuel—Environmental aspects.
3. Renewable energy sources. I. McCage, Crystal.
TP355.O38 2007
553.2'82–dc22   2006027870

Printed in the United States of America

Contents

Chapter 1: The History of Oil

Chapter 2: Does Oil Harm the Environment?

Chapter 3: Is Oil a Viable Energy Source for the Future?

Foreword

The wind farm at Altamont Pass in Northern California epitomizes many people's idea of wind power: Hundreds of towering white turbines generate electricity to power homes, factories, and businesses. The spinning turbine blades call up visions of a brighter future in which clean, renewable energy sources replace dwindling and polluting fossil fuels. The blades also kill over a thousand birds of prey each year. Every energy source, it seems, has its price.

The bird deaths at Altamont Pass make clear an unfortunate fact about all energy sources, including renewables: They have downsides. People want clean, abundant energy to power their modern lifestyles, but few want to pay the costs associated with energy production and use. Oil, coal, and natural gas contain high amounts of energy, but using them produces pollution. Commercial solar energy facilities require hundreds of acres of land and thus must be located in rural areas. Expensive and ugly transmission lines must then be run from the solar plants to the cities that need power. Producing hydrogen for fuel involves the use of dirty fossil fuels, tapping geothermal energy depletes ground water, and growing biomass for fuel ties up land that could be used to grow food. Hydroelectric power has become increasingly unpopular because dams flood vital habitats and kill wildlife and plants. Perhaps most controversial, nuclear power plants produce highly dangerous radioactive waste. People's reluctance to pay these environmental costs can be seen in the results of a 2006 Center for Economic and Civic Opinion poll. When asked how much they would support a power plant in their neighborhood, 66 percent of respondents said they would oppose it.

Many scientists warn that fossil fuel use creates emissions that threaten human health and cause global warming. Moreover, numerous scientists claim that fossil fuels are running out. As a result of these concerns, many nations have begun to revisit the energy sources that first powered human enterprises.

In his 2006 State of the Union speech, U.S. President George W. Bush announced that since 2001 the United States has spent "$10 billion to develop cleaner, cheaper, and more reliable alternative energy sources," such as biomass and wind power. Despite Bush's positive rhetoric, many critics contend that the renewable energy sources he refers to are still as inefficient as they ever were and cannot possibly power modern economies. As Jerry Taylor and Peter Van Doren of the Cato Institute note, "The market share for non-hydro renewable energy . . . has languished between 1 and 3 percent for decades." Controversies such as this have been a constant throughout the history of humanity's search for the perfect energy source.

Greenhaven Press's Fueling the Future series explores this history. Each volume in the series traces the development of one energy source, and investigates the controversies surrounding its environmental impact and its potential to power humanity's future. The anthologies provide a variety of selections written by scientists, environmental activists, industry leaders, and government experts. Volumes also contain useful research tools, including an introductory essay providing important context, and an annotated table of contents that enables students to locate selections of interest easily. In addition, each volume includes an index, chronology, bibliography, glossary, and a Facts About section, which lists useful information about each energy source. Other features include numerous charts, graphs, and cartoons, which offer additional avenues for learning important information about the topic.

Fueling the Future volumes provide students with important resources for learning about the energy sources upon which human societies depend. Although it is easy to take energy for granted in developed nations, this series emphasizes how energy sources are also problematic. The U.S. Energy Information Administration calls energy "essential to life." Whether scientists will be able to develop the energy sources necessary to sustain modern life is the vital question explored in Greenhaven Press's Fueling the Future series.

Introduction

In the 1956 film *Giant*, James Dean's character, Jett Rink, is a poor outcast in west Texas who strikes oil on a small patch of land he inherited. This event changes his life and his social status forever. Upon making the discovery, Rink tells his wealthy nemesis Bick Benedict, "My well came in big, so big. And there's more down there, bigger wells. I'm rich, Bick! I'm a rich one. I'm a rich boy."

Rink's assertion that "there's more down there" is emblematic of the long-held belief that oil will never run out. Rink's optimism has been shared by Americans since the automobile became a staple of life in the United States. With the advent of the gasoline-powered automobile in the late 1800s, America's dependence on oil was sealed. Growing car ownership inspired the nation to build an ever-increasing number of roads, which led to the growth of suburbs. Americans from all walks of life worked to purchase a home in the suburbs in order to live what many thought was the American dream.

However, as Americans moved farther away from urban centers, they began to drive longer distances to work, enforcing the nation's reliance on the automobile. This increased reliance also deepened America's dependence on oil. Unfortunately, as dependence on oil has increased, oil reserves in the United States have decreased, forcing the nation to buy an increasing percentage of its oil from other nations. This reliance comes at a cost. Importing over half of its oil from other nations, the United States is vulnerable to price shocks and supply disruptions caused by political unrest in other areas of the world, especially the Middle East. When *Giant* was made, few Americans would have believed that in less than twenty years, oil discoveries such as Rink's would be increasingly uncommon in the United States.

Marion King Hubbert Predicts an Oil Crisis

One man had already come to this conclusion, however. In the same year that *Giant* was released, geophysicist Marion King

Hubbert predicted that oil discovery in the lower forty-eight states would peak in the 1970s. He also predicted that world oil discovery would peak shortly after the year 2000. At first, not many people listened to Hubbert's predictions, but when oil discovery in the lower forty-eight states did indeed peak in the 1970s, scientists from all over the world began to examine Hubbert's predictions more closely. Many scientists have reaffirmed his prediction of a world oil shortage, whereas others say that the

The United States imports more than half of its oil from other nations, such as Kuwait where this drilling rig is situated.

peak he predicted will not occur. New technology, they say, will enable the oil industry to find and extract more oil than is now thought possible. Despite the debate over Hubbert's predictions, many governments are cautiously assuming the worst. They have begun to invest in alternative transportation fuels, such as hydrogen, that can be used in lieu of oil.

The United States, the world's largest consumer of oil, has begun such an investment. Even if Hubbert's prediction about an oil crisis turns out to be inaccurate, many experts believe that the nation should nevertheless reduce its dependence on

Many scientists believe that burning oil and other fossil fuels will increase volatile weather events such as hurricanes.

foreign oil. They claim that this reliance has had a harmful impact on the country. For example, they say that as the nation has become more dependent on other nations for oil, America's economy—which depends upon cheap transportation—has become vulnerable. To protect the U.S. economy, the federal government has involved America in conflicts around the world to ensure access to other nations' oil supplies. The 2003 war in Iraq is a good example. Despite the Bush administration's claim that the war was waged to fight terrorism, many critics contend that the war was started to gain control of Iraq's ample oil reserves. These opponents criticize the administration for invading another country just to protect American interests. Although not everyone agrees with the claim that the Iraq war was waged for oil, as the conflict in that nation continues, suspicions about America's real motives have intensified.

Environmental Concerns About Oil

In addition to concerns about U.S. involvement in foreign conflicts, worries about the environmental impact of America's oil usage have led to calls to reduce oil dependency. The negative effects of large oil spills are immediately recognizable: Most Americans are familiar with TV images of beaches covered in oil and waterfowl floundering in the sand, their feathers so coated with oil that they cannot fly. Despite the concern that these spills produce, a far bigger worry is global warming. Many scientists believe that the burning of fossil fuels such as oil produces greenhouse gases that contribute to global warming. Evidence for global warming, these experts claim, is record-high temperatures and unusually volatile weather, characterized by severe droughts and powerful hurricanes. Americans concerned about the environmental impacts of oil usage are increasingly unwilling to support increased drilling in the United States. For example, polls show that the majority of Americans are opposed to drilling for oil in the Arctic National Wildlife Refuge (ANWR), citing environmental concerns. Americans dislike the idea of spoiling the pristine beauty of the refuge and harming the animals that live there simply to obtain more oil. They believe that more drilling is not the answer to America's energy woes. More drilling would simply harm the environment for short-term gain, they contend, when what is needed is development of clean, renewable energy sources such as hydrogen.

The Future of Oil

The belief that America should transition from oil to cleaner, renewable transportation fuels is beginning to shape public policy. In his 2006 State of the Union address, President George W. Bush called for America to end its dependency on oil. He said, "Keeping America competitive requires affordable energy. And here we have a serious problem: America is addicted to oil, which is often imported from unstable parts of the world. The best way to break this addiction is through technology." He then went on to announce the Advanced Energy Initiative, which will provide a 22 percent increase in clean energy research at the U.S. Department of Energy. This research has two main goals—to change how Americans power their homes and offices and to change how the nation powers its automobiles. Bush has made investment in hydrogen a central part of his energy plan.

While many Americans applaud Bush's stance, others criticize the president for claiming that America is "addicted" to oil. They point out that Americans simply use oil because it is a good bargain. They argue that oil remains relatively inexpensive relative to the energy it provides. Some analysts go so far as to say that dependency on foreign oil is beneficial to America. Since oil in some nations is abundant, these countries sell it cheaply. Clearly, buying inexpensive oil from oil-rich nations to run America's economy is more cost-effective than investing in expensive and untried alternatives such as hydrogen, many commentators claim.

Although controversy continues over oil dependency, one thing is clear: America is more reliant on oil than ever before. While Americans claim to be concerned about the nation's dependence on oil, they continue to buy large vehicles—which consume more gasoline than do small vehicles—and commute longer distances than ever before. Fuel economy for U.S. vehicles was lower in 2002 than at any time since 1981, when oil embargos prompted carmakers to build smaller, more fuel-efficient cars. This decrease in automotive fuel efficiency is largely due to the popularity of sports utility vehicles (SUVs), which get substantially worse gas mileage than do passenger cars.

As gas prices rose in 2006, however, the popularity of SUVs dropped off slightly. During the same year, car companies offered more hybrid vehicles such as the Toyota Prius than ever before. Hybrids run on a combination of gasoline and electricity, thereby reducing overall oil consumption. Automobile manufacturers continue to work on refining a hydrogen fuel cell car, and many carmakers now sell vehicles that run on a combination of ethanol and gasoline.

Whether or not the move to smaller vehicles and the increasing popularity of hybrid cars means that Americans are finally ready to end their oil dependency remains to be seen. The nation has relied on oil for over a century, and any transition to alternative fuels would require enormous changes for the nation.

A hybrid sport utility vehicle. Increased concern about oil supply has led to the development of hybrid vehicles that save gas by running in part on electricity.

Technological advancements in hydrogen fuel cell technology would have to occur, for example, before hydrogen cars would become feasible. The transportation network that moves gasoline from refineries to filling stations would have to be completely converted in order to supply drivers with hydrogen fuel. Oil companies and car manufacturers, whose fortunes—like those of *Giant*'s Jett Rink—have been built on oil dependency, are likely to resist these changes. Perhaps more important than technology and infrastructure is the fact that Americans may have to make personal sacrifices such as driving less or paying more for hybrid vehicles. President Bush has called for increased energy conservation, but Americans are used to driving everywhere, whenever they want. Indeed, the freedom of movement provided by the automobile is central to American life. Despite the harms associated with oil, it likely will remain an essential ingredient of life in America for years to come.

CHAPTER 1

The History of Oil

The discovery of oil in the United States in 1859 was a turning point in the nation's history.

The Early Uses of Oil

Wayne M. Pafko

Wayne M. Pafko holds a bachelor of science degree in chemical engineering from the University of Minnesota. The following article is a part of his project studying the history and science of oil and oil technology, which he worked on while in college. Pafko briefly traces the history of oil, describing how it was used in ancient times for mummification, painting, and healing. He then describes the search for and discovery of oil in the United States in 1859. Pafko concludes by describing oil's importance to the U.S. economy. Pafko now works for the Procter and Gamble Company in Cincinnati, Ohio.

Small amounts of petroleum have been used throughout history. The Egyptians coated mummies and sealed their mighty Pyramids with pitch. The Babylonians, Assyrians, and Persians used it to pave their streets and hold their walls and buildings together. Boats along the Euphrates were constructed with woven reeds and sealed with pitch. The Chinese also came across it while digging holes for brine (salt water) and used the petroleum for heating. The Bible even claims that Noah used it to make his Ark seaworthy.

American Indians used petroleum for paint, fuel, and medicine. Desert nomads used it to treat camels for mange, and the Holy Roman Emperor, Charles V, used petroleum to treat his gout. Ancient Persians and Sumatrans also believed petroleum had medicinal value. This seemed a popular idea, and up through the 19th century jars of petroleum were sold as a miracle tonic able to cure whatever ailed you. People who drank

Wayne M. Pafko, "Case Study: Petroleum; Origins of the Industry," http:www.pafko.com/history/h_petro.html, 2000. Reproduced by permission.

this "snake oil" discovered that petroleum doesn't taste very good!

The Search for Oil

Yet despite its usefulness, for thousands of years petroleum was very scarce. People collected it when it bubbled to the surface or seeped into wells. For those digging wells to get drinking water the petroleum was seen as a nuisance. However, some thought the oil might have large-scale economic value. George Bissell, a lawyer, thought that petroleum might be converted into kerosene for use in lamps. An analysis by Benjamin Silliman, Jr., a Yale chemistry and geology professor, confirmed his hunch.

In 1854 Bissell and a friend formed the unsuccessful Pennsylvania Rock Oil Company. Not one to be easily dismayed, in 1858 Bissell and a group of business men formed the Seneca Oil Company. They hired an ex-railroad conductor named Edwin Drake to drill for oil along a secluded creek in Titusville, Pennsylvania. They soon dubbed him "Colonel" Drake to impress the locals. But the "Colonel" needed help so he hired Uncle Billy Smith and his two sons who had experience with drilling salt wells. In 1859 this motley crew found oil at a depth of 69 1/2 feet.

Pennsylvania's "Black Gold"

Drake's well produced only thirty-five barrels a day; however, he could sell it for $20 a barrel. News of the well quickly spread and brought droves of fortune seekers. Soon the hills were covered with prospectors trying to decide where to dig their wells. Some used Y-shaped divining rods to guide them. Others followed Drake's lead and drilled close to water, a technique that was dubbed "creekology". Many found oil, but usually at 4 or 5 hundred feet below the surface. Drake had just been lucky to find oil so high up!

To dig the wells, six-inch-wide cast iron pipes were sunk down to the bedrock. A screw-like drill was then used to scoop out dirt and rock from the middle. Many discovered to their dismay that once they hit oil they had no way to contain all of it. Until caps were added to the wells, vast quantities of oil flowed into the appropriately named Oil Creek.

The First Pipeline

Transporting the oil was also a problem. In 1865 Samuel Van Syckel, an oil buyer, began construction on a two-inch wide pipeline designed to span the distance to the railroad depot five miles away. The teamsters, who had previously transported the oil, didn't take too kindly to Syckel's plan, and they used pick-axes to break apart the line. Eventually Van Syckel brought in armed guards, finished the pipeline, and made a ton of money. By 1865 wooden derricks bled 3.5 million barrels a year out of the ground. Such large scale production caused the price of crude oil to plummet to ten cents a barrel.

How Much Oil?

Andrew Carnegie was a large stockholder in the Columbia Oil Company. Carnegie believed that the oil fields would quickly run dry because of all the drilling. He persuaded Columbia Oil to dig a huge hole to store 100,000 barrels of oil so that they could make a killing when the country's wells went dry. Luckily there was more oil than they thought! But don't feel too sorry for Carnegie; he didn't let the setback slow him down very much and went on to make his millions in the steel industry.

In contrast, "Colonel" Drake was committed to the oil business. He scoured the country looking for customers willing to buy his crude oil. However, the bad smell, muddy black color, and highly volatile component, called naphtha, caused few sales. It became obvious that one would have to refine the oil to find a market.

Early Refining

By 1860 there were 15 refineries in operation. Known as "tea kettle" stills, they consisted of a large iron drum and a long tube which acted as a condenser. Capacity of these stills ranged from 1 to 100 barrels a day. A coal fire heated the drum, and three fractions were obtained during the distillation process. The first component to boil off was the highly volatile naphtha. Next came the kerosene, or "lamp oil", and lastly came the heavy oils and tar which were simply left in the bottom of the drum. These early refineries produced about 75% kerosene, which could be sold for high profits.

Early oil wells produced foul-smelling, messy, crude oil that did not find immediate success in the marketplace.

Kerosene was so valuable because of a whale shortage that had began in 1845 due to heavy hunting. Sperm [whale] oil had been the main product of the whaling industry and was used in lamps. Candles were made with another whale product called "spermaceti". This shortage of natural sources meant that kerosene was in great demand. Almost all the families across the country started using kerosene to light their homes. However, the naphtha and tar fractions were seen as valueless and were simply dumped into Oil Creek. . . .

Later these waste streams were converted into valuable products. In 1869 Robert Chesebrough discovered how to make petroleum jelly and called his new product Vaseline. The heavy components began being used as lubricants, or as waxes

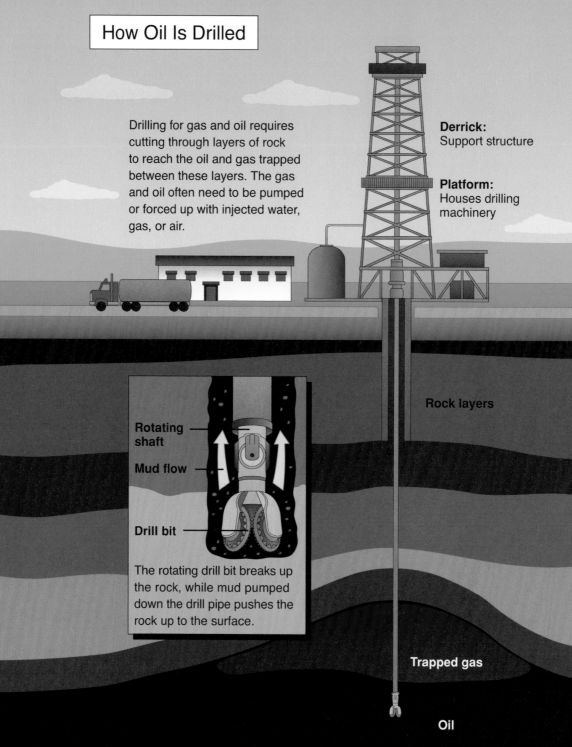

How Oil Is Drilled

Drilling for gas and oil requires cutting through layers of rock to reach the oil and gas trapped between these layers. The gas and oil often need to be pumped or forced up with injected water, gas, or air.

Derrick: Support structure

Platform: Houses drilling machinery

Rock layers

Rotating shaft

Mud flow

Drill bit

The rotating drill bit breaks up the rock, while mud pumped down the drill pipe pushes the rock up to the surface.

Trapped gas

Oil

Source: Ian Graham, *Fossil Fuels*, 1990

in candles and chewing gum. Tar was used as a roofing material. But the more volatile components were still without much value. Limited success came in using gasoline as a local anesthetic and liquid petroleum gas (LPG) in a compression cycle to make ice. The success in refined petroleum products greatly spread the technique. By 1865 there were 194 refineries in operation.

John D. Rockefeller Enters the Oil Market

In 1862 John D. Rockefeller financed his first refinery as a side investment. He soon discovered that he liked the petroleum industry, and devoted himself to it full time. As a young bookkeeper Rockefeller had come to love the order of a well organized ledger. However, he was appalled by the disorder and instability of the oil industry. Anyone could drill a well, and overproduction plagued the early industry. At times this overproduction meant that the crude oil was cheaper than water. Rockefeller saw early on that refining and transportation, as opposed to production, were the keys to taking control of the industry. And control the industry he did!

In 1870 he established Standard Oil, which then controlled 10% of the refining capacity in the country. Transportation often encompassed 20% of the total production cost, and Rockefeller made under-the-table deals with railroads to give him secret shipping rebates. This cheap transportation allowed Standard to undercut its competitors, and Rockefeller expanded aggressively, buying out

By 1880, the Standard Oil company controlled 90 percent of the oil market in the U.S., making John D. Rockefeller the richest man in the world.

competitors left and right. Soon Standard built a network of "iron arteries" which delivered oil across the Eastern U.S. This pipeline system relieved Standard's dependence upon the railroads and reduced its transportation costs even more. By 1880 Standard controlled 90% of the country's refining capacity. Because of its massive size, it brought security and stability to the oil business, guaranteeing continuous profits. With Standard Oil, John D. Rockefeller became the richest person in the world.

Significance of Oil Discovery in the United States

But what came out of all this activity? In short the early petroleum industry:

- Brought a revolution in lighting with kerosene
- Helped keep machines in good condition with lubricants (It was the "Machine Age" after all)
- Provided a new source of national wealth (In 1865 it was the country's 6th largest export)
- Aided the Union in the Civil War by strengthening the economy (Also petroleum was used to treat wounded soldiers at the battle of Gettysburg).

The Construction of the First Oil Well

Brian Black

> In the following selection Brian Black, associate professor
> of history and environmental studies at Pennsylvania State
> University, describes how Edwin Drake built the first oil
> well in Pennsylvania in 1859. When Drake was hired in
> 1858, he struggled to find men who would work for him;
> many thought his idea that he could obtain large quantities
> of oil by drilling into the earth was insane. But Drake finally
> succeeded in hiring a blacksmith to do the job. When Drake
> lost funding for his project, he took out his own line of
> credit, and on August 28, 1859, Drake's well produced oil.

Dr. Francis Brewer traveled to Titusville [Pennsylvania] in
1851 in such an atmosphere of economic expansion. As a
practicing physician in Vermont, he had two years earlier received a barrel of five gallons of creek oil from his father in Titusville. He became a believer in its medicinal use and often
prescribed it to patients. While wandering about his family's
lumber holdings in this remote section of the state, Brewer took
time to examine a well-known oil spring. Before leaving Titusville for his home, Brewer formally contracted a local man, J.
D. Angier, to collect the oil that he noted seeping to the surface. It was the first oil lease ever signed; however, there was
still no effort to drill into the earth for the substance. Angier instead dug trenches to convey oil and water to a central basin,

where some crude machinery separated the two wells enough to produce three or four gallons of oil a day. Here, then, begins the astounding sequence of chance occurrences that brought Pennsylvania rock oil to market.

The Project Begins

Upon his return to Vermont, Brewer took with him a bottle of the oil. The proverbial genie was escaping the bottle. Dixi Crosby, a chemist at Dartmouth College, acquired the sample and shared it with a young businessman, George Bissell, who happened to be visiting his alma mater. Bissell worked in the coal oil business, and the sample immediately struck him as similar. Crosby soon traveled with Brewer to Titusville to examine the spring firsthand. Dr. Brewer later described this moment:

> As we stood on the circle of rough logs, surrounding the spring, and saw the oil bubbling up, and spreading its bright and golden colors over the surface, Crosby at once proposed to purchase the whole [McClintock] farm, which we could have done for $7,000, but [there was] not enough money. When I told Crosby that we [Brewer, Watson and Co.] did not want to take money from the lumber business to put into oil, Crosby said, "damn lumber, I would rather have McClintock's farm than all the timber in Western Pennsylvania."

Upon their return Brewer signed a lease with Bissell to develop the oil occurring on the lumber company's tract of land. The lease, however, was contingent on Bissell's locating financial backing of $250,000.

Bissell began contacting financiers to help support the project. Although each one recognized the oil's potential, they demanded more scientific verification. Even during this age of giddy expansion, the vague promise of money was not enough to attract most speculators. Bissell contracted with Benjamin Silliman Jr., of Yale University, to analyze the substance. In April 1855, Silliman released a report in which he estimated that at least 50 percent of the crude could be distilled into a satisfactory illuminant for use in camphene lamps and 90 percent in the form of distilled products holding commercial promise. Bissell's effort to raise funding suddenly became much easier.

On September 18, 1855, Bissell incorporated the Pennsylvania Rock Oil Company of Connecticut, a corporation founded solely on speculating with the potential value of the oil occurring naturally beneath and around the Oil Creek valley. The value of the valley and its contents began shifting toward an entirely new and unique frame of reference. The process of commodification transformed a nuisance—the oil that seeped into farm land and salt wells—into a product of such value that it would revolutionize life in the Oil Creek valley.

As the story goes, the summer of 1856 brought Bissell a chance look at one of Samuel Kier's handbills, which explained how he brought the oil up from below the earth's surface with salt water. Ironically, Kier included such an explanation only to stir enthusiasm among his prospective users; he had no proof of the geological occurrence of petroleum. This mystery had, however, caught the eye of the Pennsylvania Rock Oil Company of Connecticut.

Edwin Drake Joins the Effort

When James M. Townsend, a New Haven banker, succeeded Bissell as president of the corporation in 1857, he contacted [the eccentric] Edwin L. Drake, of the New Haven Railroad, about traveling to Titusville and overseeing an effort to drill for crude. One of the few facts of this tale about which there is no disagreement is the lack of any reasonable rationale for Townsend's selection of Drake.

Once Drake had arrived in Titusville, Dr. Brewer took him to the site of the spring, where, Drake would later report, "within ten minutes after my arrival upon the ground . . . I had made up my mind that it [petroleum] could be obtained in large quantities by Boreing as for Salt Water. I also

Edwin Drake, pioneer of the American oil industry.

determined that I should be the one to do it." While it is not verifiable who actually came up with the plan to drill for the oil, the thought occurred to Townsend, Bissell, or Drake at some point during the next year.

On March 23, 1858, Townsend reformed the company as the Seneca Oil Company of Connecticut. Drake brought his family to Titusville in May and began a string of unsuccessful and costly attempts to secure a blacksmith who would drill the well. Drake spent weeks combing Titusville and then the surrounding towns in search of help with his project. Men were not willing "to work for a lunatic," he remembers in an 1879 account. Refused at every turn, Drake finally traveled a hundred miles away and found a salt borer with whom he entered into a contract for a thousand feet of boring. Drake then returned to Titusville and waited for his employee—but to no avail. It turns out that the man thought the easiest way to get rid of Drake was to make a contract and pretend to come. Another hired hand died en route. As Drake faced the approaching winter in October, he decided to wait until spring to continue the experiment.

When spring arrived, it brought Drake his first hopeful return. A contact he had made in Tarentum, over a hundred miles away, sent one of his own employees to assist with the drilling. William A. Smith, a trained blacksmith who had also been involved in boring for salt, arrived in April 1859. By Smith's account, Drake asked him what he thought the operation's chances were. "Very good," Smith reports that he replied. "I would not be afraid to guarantee . . . ten barrels a day. [Drake] said, stop! half that will satisfy me."

Drake's Persistence Pays Off

Smith's account of assuring Drake that drilling would be successful remains extremely dubious, considering the widespread regional perception of Drake as a lunatic. Drake's own story is also difficult to trust or verify. However, it is obvious from every account that Drake repeatedly displayed a degree of patience beyond the normal. Again and again, the piping broke off and Drake drove forty miles by wagon to Erie for more. And then there were the relentless local hecklers. Smith drilled the first well for oil amid frequent catcalls from townspeople who had ventured out from Titusville.

Even before drilling, Drake and Smith immediately began cribbing the sixteen-foot hole that had been dug over the oil spring. After experiencing frustration with water entering the hole from the creek, one of the two men decided not to crib the hole any more but only to drive an iron pipe the rest of the way and begin drilling. Before long the novelty of the project had worn off for Drake and Smith, for the townspeople, and,

The first commercial oil well in the United States was built in Pennsylvania in 1859.

worse yet, for the investors in New Haven. During the late summer of 1859, Drake ran out of funds and wired to New Haven for more money. They offered only funds for a trip home—the Seneca Oil Company was done supporting him in this folly. Drake, showing remarkable courage, took out a line of credit locally and decided to stay on for a bit longer. He wrote Townsend, "You all feel different from what I do. You all have your legitimate business which has not been interrupted by the operation, which I staked everything I had upon the project and now find myself out of business and out of money." Drake's heartrending note reflects his desperation to succeed in this endeavor. It would be a similar sentiment that brought the string of boomers following his success. On August 27, the drill dropped five feet after one kick, evidently breaking through some sort of underground crust.

As is the case with many moments of historical importance, when the well came in—which is a misnomer for a seeping well such as this, not a flowing one—there was actually no one in attendance. Ever pious, Drake stopped drilling on August 27 to observe the Sabbath. He returned to Titusville while Smith remained. The engine house had been split by a wall and the Smith family made the single room its home, so Uncle Billy, as he was called, never truly took a day off from the site.

On Sunday, August 28, 1859, Uncle Billy and his son, Samuel, checked the well site for any changes. A dark green substance with a yellow tinge floated freely around the wellhead. Uncle Billy crouched there with Samuel and lowered a piece of tin rain spouting down the narrow pipe. The future of the valley was held in this improvised ladle as it wobbled through the piping back to the surface. Uncle Billy peered into the tin ladle and saw only a dirty, greenish grease. He had no doubt as to what he had just discovered: for the first time in human history, oil had been intentionally struck beneath the earth's surface. Drake was called from town; when he arrived, Smith called to him, "Look at this!" Drake approached and then asked, "What is that?" Smith responded, "That, Mr. Drake, is your fortune!"

How America's Fascination with Cars Led to Oil Dependence

Matthew Yeomans

In the following article freelance journalist Matthew Yeomans traces the development of the auto industry and explains how the oil industry grew alongside of it. He describes how America's fascination with the automobile began at the turn of the twentieth century with Henry Ford's invention of the Model T. As cars grew more popular, the need for gasoline grew. The oil industry responded by improving refining methods and building refueling stations. Yeomans also reports that as more cars were built, the U.S. government constructed more roads to accommodate them. The majority of these roads were built outside cities, leading to the increased development of suburbs. Thus, Yeomans concludes, the automobile and oil industries changed the face of America.

Oil and automobiles fell into each other's arms. When Gotlieb Daimler introduced the first gasoline-powered horseless carriage in 1885, the oil industry—including Standard Oil—was reeling from a body blow. Three years before, Thomas Edison had introduced electric-powered light to New York and made kerosene, the oil industry's raison d'être, essentially redundant.

Matthew Yeomans, *Oil: Anatomy of an Industry*, New York: The New Press, 2004.
© 2004 by Matthew Yeomans. Reproduced by permission of the New Press,
www.thenewpress.com (800) 233-4830.

Salvation for the oil industry would come from another new invention and, ironically, it would have one of Edison's own employees to thank for it. Henry Ford was an engineer at Edison Illuminating Company in Detroit who was obsessed with the new horseless carriage, or automobile, as it was known. In 1896 he had succeeded in constructing a gasoline-powered quadricycle and that prompted him to think of building a bigger and better automobile.

While Ford was tinkering with his invention, the early automobiles were embarking on a bumpy road to public acceptance. In Europe, the first automobile race from Paris to Bordeaux and back again had won plaudits from the public but when Narrangansett, Rhode Island, hosted its own auto race in 1896, it was

Henry Ford sits in the 1896 car, the Quadricycle. Ford's pioneering efforts made the automobile accessible to the public.

so tedious that one spectator cried "Get a horse" in frustration. Motor cars were slow, smelly, and uncomfortable, but they also were considered very sophisticated by America's upper class. By 1900, there were a few thousand on America's roads and automobile inventors were experimenting with steam-driven and electric vehicles.

Henry Ford, however, was a firm believer in gasoline and in 1908, five years after forming the Ford Motor Company, Ford and his coterie of engineers (Ford's master talent was salesmanship and leadership rather than engineering) unveiled his first gasoline-powered motorcar, the Model T.

It changed everything—the auto industry, the oil industry, the United States and, in turn, the world. Not only was the Model T a reliable, well-designed motorcar—it boasted a powerful four-cylinder engine and a wheelbase that cleared America's rutted roads—but it democratized driving in America. Until the Model T arrived, owning a car had been a luxury. Ford manufactured a motorcar for the people. . . .

Automobiles Become a Part of American Life

By 1920, some two million new cars were being sold each year and America's passion for driving mirrored its post–World War exuberances—*Fordismus* is how the Germans referred to the American giddiness in what we know as the roaring twenties. At the time, local, state, and the federal government were all making sure the automobile would have the road infrastructure it needed to succeed. Much as the introduction of Baron Haussmann's boulevards had brought a sense of space and order to nineteenth-century Paris (while conveniently demolishing the cramped city streets that had been perfect for erecting barricades), so advocates of America's City Beautiful movement envisioned wide new paved roads as the way to bring structure and elegance to the overcrowded cities. But as we now know, wider roads simply begat more automobiles and a new form of city congestion. Not that cars were blamed. It was the trolley car with its fixed route and schedule that took the fall. Mass transit, it was agreed, created gridlock and crushed the free spirit of automotive travel.

In 1929 the last section of highway stretching from Mexico to Canada opened. Expansion of the highways allowed people to live farther from their workplaces.

The motorcar's charm lay in the opportunities it gave Americans to explore the nation. Urban planners soon began planning new, elegant thoroughfares to sweep motorists out of the cities. Los Angeles's Arroyo Seco Parkway and the Grand Concourse in the Bronx were two early forerunners of the modern highway. In 1916, President Woodrow Wilson signed the Federal-Aid Highway Act, providing $75 million over five years for a highway department in every U.S. state. There were over three and a half million cars on the road by now and the act was supported both by farm groups and, tellingly, a growing movement of suburban realtors. The push to flee the cities had begun.

Through the 1920s, new highway investment across the country reached a billion dollars a year and provided the foundation for the automobile and domestic oil industry. The four-lane Bronx River Parkway opened in 1925 and asphalt fever soon captured the imagination of engineers and city planners. At the vanguard of this movement was Robert Moses. As parks commissioner for New York City, and later as near-omnipotent head of the Metropolitan Transit Authority, he would create elegant asphalt tentacles out of the city in the shape of the Saw Mill River Parkway and the Hutchinson River Parkway before later forcing his autocratic auto vision on the city itself, leveling whole neighborhoods to build the Brooklyn-Queens and Cross Bronx Expressways.

The new roads made living outside the city attractive. Not only was the price of real estate cheaper on the edges of the city, but there was, of course, more space—not least to park one's car. The notion of city suburb had been pioneered by the streetcar, which had been quietly expanding the boundaries of metropolitan living since the turn of the century. Now the motorcar blew the idea of city limits apart. The 1920s saw a 59 percent growth in suburban populations as new auto-inspired communities like Grosse Point outside of Detroit and Elmwood Park near Chicago flourished.

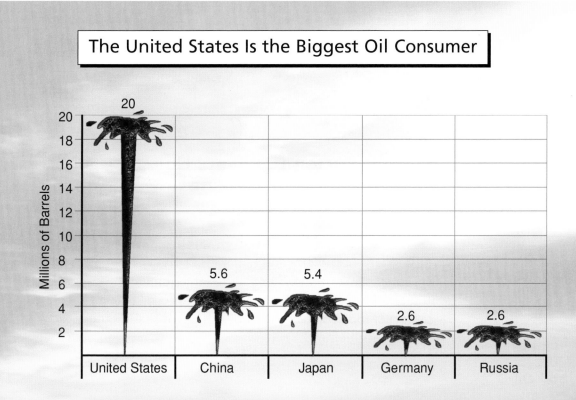

The investment in creating a new mobile American way of life would come to a halt with the 1929 stock market collapse and the onset of the Great Depression. But that didn't mean the cars stopped running. "America was the only nation in the world that ever went to the poorhouse in an automobile," Will Rogers joked at the time, and somehow the mass unemployed, like John Steinbeck's plucky Joad family in *The Grapes of Wrath*, always found a little something extra to keep their cars on the road. Standard Oil even began selling a new bottom-of-the-barrel "fighting" brand of gasoline, Stanolind Blue, for just 12¢ cents a gallon to keep America on the move. The reason was simple— the car had not just increased mobility for sight-seeing, it greatly expanded the chance of finding a job. From now on, U.S. workers would think nothing of uprooting family and moving sometimes thousands of miles across the country for new work. This new American fluidity would be an enormous asset to the U.S. economy in the years immediately following World War II, when a ready and eager mobile workforce decamped from the Northeast to the Southwest in search of new opportunities.

Just as the United States was at its lowest ebb, the automobile received its biggest push. In 1932, Franklin Delano Roosevelt promised his New Deal, a centerpiece of which was the construction of new roads. As part of the emergency Public Works Administration initiatives, one million people were hired for highway projects. FDR's Civic Works Administration allowed for 500,000 miles of road building and some 80 percent of all New Deal agency expenditures were dedicated to roads and new construction. . . .

William Burton Discovers How to Produce More Gasoline

One year after Ford's Model T went on sale, a Standard Oil executive, anticipating the need for more gasoline, began fashioning a solution. William Burton was head of manufacturing at Standard of Indiana and had a Ph.D. in chemistry. His aim was to crack—or break down—the larger molecules contained in fuel oil by heating them under high pressure up to 650 degrees to produce more gasoline. By 1913, his first thermal cracking still, producing 45 percent gasoline from a barrel of crude, went into operation just as gasoline sales in the U.S. overtook those of kerosene.

Burton's invention ensured there would be enough gasoline to satisfy the car-crazy public. But that still left the question of how the oil companies would get the gasoline to the consumer. By 1914, Socal [Standard Oil of California] had thirty-four standardized filling stations in California, but most gasoline was still sold by mom-and-pop general stores and other miscellaneous businesses. The oil companies continued to recruit small businesses as new outlets for selling gasoline because it meant they didn't have to invest in new buildings and could reap a quick profit. Soon, gasoline pumps were cropping up outside any curbside business that wanted them, with little regulation on the quality of gasoline sold or how safely it was dispensed. It took a series of gas fires and explosions at these often overcrowded and

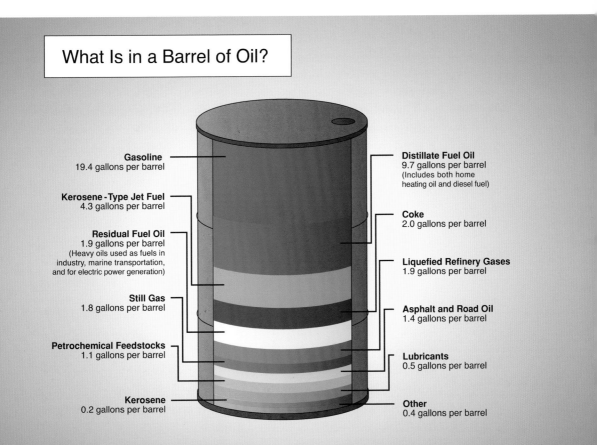

What Is in a Barrel of Oil?

Gasoline
19.4 gallons per barrel

Kerosene - Type Jet Fuel
4.3 gallons per barrel

Residual Fuel Oil
1.9 gallons per barrel
(Heavy oils used as fuels in industry, marine transportation, and for electric power generation)

Still Gas
1.8 gallons per barrel

Petrochemical Feedstocks
1.1 gallons per barrel

Kerosene
0.2 gallons per barrel

Distillate Fuel Oil
9.7 gallons per barrel
(Includes both home heating oil and diesel fuel)

Coke
2.0 gallons per barrel

Liquefied Refinery Gases
1.9 gallons per barrel

Asphalt and Road Oil
1.4 gallons per barrel

Lubricants
0.5 gallons per barrel

Other
0.4 gallons per barrel

(Note: Figures are based on average yields for U.S. refineries in 2000. One barrel contains 42 gallons of crude oil. (Source: API))

Source: Matthew Yeomans, *Oil: Anatomy of an Industry*, 2004

poorly maintained pumps to prompt local government to begin zoning where gasoline could be sold and what structure was required to house the gasoline tanks.

This gasoline free-for-all was also hurting the oil companies' brand image and that was increasingly important as oil prices plummeted and the companies had to compete harder against each other. Their solution was to construct stand-alone gasoline emporiums—service stations, as they were called east of the Rockies, and filling stations, as [Socal's area manager John] McClean had coined them, to the west. Some 143,000 drive-in gas stations had been built by 1929 and, to identify and market their brands, the companies devised logos that they hung high throughout the nation for passing motorists to see. The companies also aggressively marketed new types of "improved gasoline" that promised better performance than their competitors'; some even colored their gas with blue and red dyes to help build brand recognition. Drivers quickly came to identify with the brand they could trust, be it the star of Texaco, the dinosaur of Sinclair, Shell's scallop shell, or Socony's Pegasus. This loyalty might remain for years and be passed down through the family from father to son. Driving, after all, was still very much a male domain.

The oil companies were also selling something more intoxicating than the fumes of gasoline. They offered their customers a sense of freedom they had never experienced before. And, with so many of the new middle class driving the same Model T car, the different gasolines offered a whiff of individuality, a far cry from the communal drudge of the Old World.

In 1928 advertising icon Bruce Barton delivered a messianic speech to a gathering of top oil executives. Brand awareness was already a buzzword through the industry but Barton wanted his audience to understand something higher—the "magic of gasoline."

"It is the juice of the fountain of youth that you are selling," he told them. "It is health. It is comfort. It is success. And you have sold merely a bad smelling liquid at so many cents per gallon. . . . There is a magnificent place for imagination in your business, but you must get it on the other side of the pump. You must put yourself in the place of the man and woman in whose lives your gasoline has worked miracles."

Marion King Hubbert Predicts the End of the Oil Age

David Goodstein

In this selection, David Goodstein, professor of physics at the California Institute of Technology, examines geophysicist Marion King Hubbert's prediction of an oil shortage. Goodstein explains how an improvement in most people's standard of living in the twentieth century increased worldwide demand for oil. According to Goodstein, up until the 1950s, geologists thought that the supply of oil would be infinite; however, in 1956 Hubbert predicted that the extraction of oil from the lower forty-eight states would peak around 1970. When this prediction was found to be accurate, other oil geologists began to take a closer look at all of Hubbert's predictions. Using Hubbert's methods, many scientists now predict that the peak in world oil extraction is perhaps only a few years away.

In the 1950s, the United States was the world's leading producer of oil. Much of the nation's industrial and military might derived from its giant oil industry. The country seemed to be floating on a rich, gooey ocean of "black gold." Nobody was willing to believe that the party would ever end. Well, almost nobody. There was a geophysicist named Marion King Hubbert who knew better.

Hubbert, the son of a central Texas farm family, was born in 1903. Somehow he wound up at the far-off University of Chicago, where he earned all his academic degrees right up to the Ph.D. Embittered with the academic world after an unhappy stint teaching geophysics at Columbia University, he spent the bulk of his professional career with the Shell Oil Company of Houston. That's where he was when, in 1956, very much against the will of his employer, he made public his calculation that American oil dominance would soon come to an end. To understand how he reached that conclusion and the relevance of his reasoning to world oil supplies today, we need to understand a bit about how oil came to be in the first place.

How Oil Is Formed

For hundreds of millions of years, animal, vegetable, and mineral matter drifted downward through the waters to settle on the floors of ancient seas. In a few privileged places on Earth, strata of porous rock formed that were particularly rich in organic inclusions. With time, these strata were buried deep beneath the seabed. The interior of Earth is hot, heated by the decay of natural radioactive elements. If the porous source rock sank just deep enough, it reached the proper temperature for the organic matter to be transformed into oil. Then the weight of the rock above it could squeeze the oil out of the source rock like water out of a sponge, into layers above and below, where it could be trapped. Over vast stretches of time, in various parts of the globe, the seas retreated, leaving some of those deposits beneath the surface of the land.

Oil consists of long-chain hydrocarbon molecules. If the source rock sank too deep, the excessive heat at greater depths—some three miles below the surface—broke these long molecules into the shorter hydrocarbon molecules we call natural gas. Meanwhile, in certain swampy places, the decay of dead plant matter created peat bogs. In the course of the eons, buried under sediments and heated by Earth's interior, the peat was transformed into coal, a substance that consists mostly of elemental carbon. Coal, oil, and natural gas are the primary fossil fuels. They are energy from the Sun, stored within the earth.

How Oil Is Formed

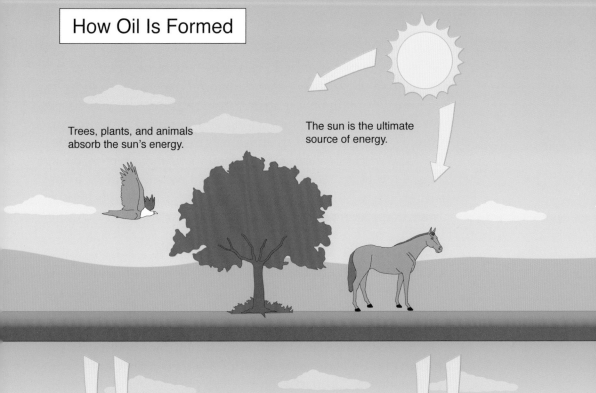

The sun is the ultimate source of energy.

Trees, plants, and animals absorb the sun's energy.

Over the years, the remains of trees, plants, and animals become covered with layers of sand and silt.

Heat and enormous pressure from these layers compress the remains and convert the long-stored sun's energy into oil and gas.

Source: Ian Graham, *Fossil Fuels*, 1990

Until only two hundred years ago—the blink of an eye on the scale of our history—the human race was able to live almost entirely on light as it arrived from the Sun. The Sun nourished plants, which provided food and warmth for us and our animals. It illuminated the day and (in most places) left the night sky, sparkling with stars, to comfort us in our repose. Back then, a few people in the civilized world traveled widely, even sailing across the oceans, but most people probably never strayed very far from their birthplaces. . . .

Humanity's Dependency on Oil

Today we who live in the developed world expect illumination at night and air conditioning in summer. We may work every day up to a hundred miles from where we live, depending on multiton individual vehicles to transport us back and forth on demand, on roads paved with asphalt (another by-product of the age of oil). Thousands of airline flights per day can take us to virtually any destination on Earth in a matter of hours. When we get there, we can still chat with our friends and family back home, or conduct business as if we had never left the office. Amenities that were once reserved for the rich are available to most people, refrigeration rather than spices preserves food, and machines do much of our hard labor. Ships, planes, trains, and trucks transport goods of every description all around the world. Earth's population exceeds six billion people. We don't see the stars so clearly anymore, but on most counts few of us would choose to return to the eighteenth century. . . .

Hubbert's Prediction

Throughout the twentieth century, the demand for and supply of oil grew rapidly. Those two are essentially equal. Oil is always used as fast as it's pumped out of the ground. Until the 1950s, oil geologists entertained the mathematically impossible expectation that the same rate of increase could continue forever. All warnings of finite supplies were hooted down, because new reserves were being discovered faster than consumption was rising. Then, in 1956, Hubbert predicted that the rate at which oil could be extracted from the lower forty-eight United States would peak around 1970 and decline rapidly after that.

When his prediction was borne out, other oil geologists started paying serious attention.

Hubbert used a number of methods to do his calculations. The first was similar to ideas that had been used by population biologists for well over a century. When a new population—of humans or any other species—starts growing in an area that has abundant resources, the growth is initially exponential, which means that the rate of growth increases by the same fraction each year, like compound interest in a bank account. That is just how the geologists used to think oil discovery would grow. However, once the population is big enough so that the resources no longer seem unlimited, the rate of growth starts slowing down. The same happens with oil discovery, because the chances of finding new oil get smaller when there's less new oil to find. Hubbert showed that once the rate of increase of oil discovery starts to decline, it's possible to extrapolate the declining rate to find where growth will stop altogether. At that point, all the oil in the ground has been discovered, and the total amount there ever was is equal to the amount that's already been used plus the known reserves still in the ground. Hubbert noticed that the trend of declining annual rate of increase of oil discovery was established for the lower forty-eight

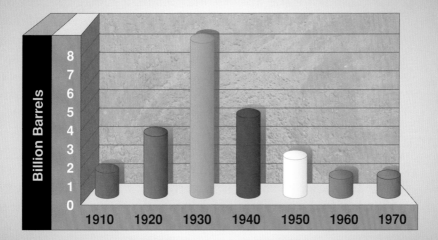

Discovery Dates of U.S. Oil Fields

Billion Barrels

1910   1920   1930   1940   1950   1960   1970

Source: David Goodstein, *Out of Gas: The End of the Age of Oil*, 2004

All Oil Production Will Peak

"Formulated by Shell Oil geophysicist M. King Hubbert, 'peak oil' is the recognition that oil and gas are finite resources subject to depletion. All oil production will peak according to a bell curve, with increasingly negative repercussions after the peak, when supply plummets and demand increases. Hubbert, who died in 1989, was mostly ignored in 1956 when he predicted continental U.S. oil production would crest between 1965 and 1970. But when domestic production peaked in 1970, experts applied his suddenly portentous theory to world supplies. Various Hubbertites now predict that global oil production will peak within twenty years."

Robert Thompson, *Esquire*, October 2005.

states by the 1950s. Others have now pointed out that the rate of discovery worldwide has been declining for decades. The total quantity of conventional oil that Earth stored up for us is estimated by this method to be about two trillion barrels.

Hubbert's second method required assuming that in the long run, when the historical record of the rate at which oil was pumped out of the ground was plotted, it would be a bell-shaped curve. That is, it would first rise (as it has been), then reach a peak that would never be exceeded, and afterward decline forever. Now that it's far enough along, half a century after he made that assumption, it's clear that he was right in the case of the lower forty-eight. If the same assumption is correct for the rest of the world, and if you have the historical record of the rising part of the curve and a good estimate of the total amount of oil that ever was (two trillion barrels, see above), then it's not difficult to predict when the peak, Hubbert's peak, will occur. Hubbert had that information in the 1950s for the lower forty-eight. We have it now for the whole world. Different geologists using different data and methods get slightly different results, but some (not all) have concluded that the peak will happen at some point in this decade. The point can be seen without any fancy mathematics at all. Of the two trillion barrels of oil we started with, nearly half has already been consumed. The peak occurs when we reach the halfway point. That, they say, can't be more than a few years off.

Hubbert's third method applied the observation that the total amount of oil extracted to date paralleled oil discovery but lagged behind by a few decades. In other words, we pump oil out of the ground at about the same rate that we discover it, but a few decades later. Thus the rate of discovery predicts the rate of extraction. Worldwide, remember, the rate of discovery started declining decades ago. In other words, Hubbert's peak for oil discovery already occurred, decades ago. That gives an independent prediction of when Hubbert's peak for oil consumption will occur. It will occur, according to that method, within the next decade or so.

Some Scientists Disagree

Not all geologists pay attention to this assessment. Many prefer to take the total amount known for sure to be in the ground and divide that by the rate at which it's getting used up. This is known in the industry as the R/P ratio—that is, the ratio of reserves to production. Depending on what data one uses, the R/P ratio is currently between forty and a hundred years. They conclude that if we continue to pump oil out of the ground and consume it at the same rate we are doing now, we will not have pumped the last drop for another forty to one hundred years.

Another point of disagreement concerns the total amount of oil that nature has produced on Earth. Over the period 1995–2000, the United States Geological Survey (USGS) made an exhaustive study of worldwide oil supplies. The resulting

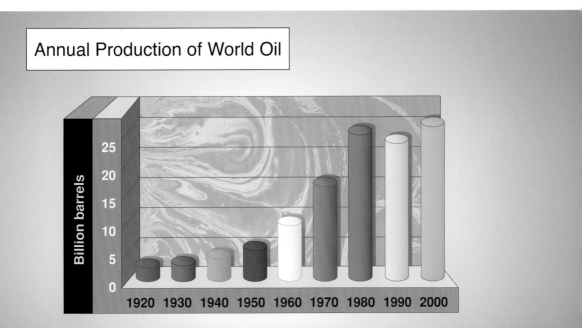

Source: David Goodstein, *Out of Gas: The End of the Age of Oil*, 2004

report concludes that, with 95 percent certainty, there was the equivalent of at least two trillion barrels when we started pumping. However, it also concludes with 50 percent probability that there were at least 2.7 trillion barrels—based on the expectation that, contrary to trends mentioned earlier, new discovery will continue at a brisk rate for at least thirty more years. The additional 0.7 trillion barrels to be unearthed would amount to discovering all over again all the oil that's now known to exist in the Middle East. . . .

Reasons for Concern

Nevertheless, all our experience with the consumption of natural resources suggests that the rate at which we use them up starts at zero, rises to a peak that will never be exceeded, and then declines back to zero as the supply becomes exhausted. There have been many instances of that behavior: coal mining in Pennsylvania, copper in northern Michigan, and many others, including oil in the lower forty-eight. That picture forms the fundamental basis of the views of Hubbert and his followers, but it is ignored by those who depend on the R/P ratio. Given that worldwide demand will continue to increase, as it has for well over a century, Hubbert's followers expect the crisis to occur when the peak is reached, rather than when the last drop is pumped. In other words, we will be in trouble when we've used up half the oil that existed, not all of it.

Oil's effect on the environment is a topic of great controversy.

CHAPTER 2

Does Oil Harm the Environment?

The Burning of Oil Causes Global Warming

Ross Gelbspan

> Ross Gelbspan, a Pulitzer Prize–winning reporter, claims that new research has proven the seriousness of climate change. He lists several events that underscore how serious global warming has become, including pandemics and falling food production. Gelbspan argues that developed nations must reduce their use of fossil fuels such as oil by transitioning to clean, renewable energy sources.

"We've known for some time that we have to worry about the impacts of climate change on our children's and grandchildren's generations. But we now have to worry about ourselves as well."
—*Margaret Beckett, British secretary of state for environment, April 26, 2002*

By late 2003, the signals were undeniable: Global climate change is threatening to spiral out of control.

The six-month period from June to December 2003 brought a succession of scientific findings, climate impacts, political and diplomatic developments, and responses from the financial world that vividly underscored the urgency and magnitude of the climate crisis.

Ross Gelbspan, *Boiling Point: How Politicians, Big Oil and Coal, Journalists, and Activists Are Fueling the Climate Crisis—and What We Can Do to Avert Disaster*. New York: Basic Books, 2004. Copyright © 2004 by Ross Gelbspan. Reprinted by permission of Basic Books, a member of Perseus Books, L.L.C.

The events of that year surprised even many seasoned climate scientists—and brought home to many others the fact that, given all its ramifications, the climate crisis is far more than just an environmental issue. It is a civilizational issue.

Nevertheless, by the end of 2003, most Americans were still in denial.

Evidence of Global Warming

The evidence is not subtle. It is apparent in the trickling meltwater from the glaciers in the Andes Mountains that will soon leave many people on Bolivia's mountainside villages with no water to irrigate their crops and, after that, not even enough to drink. It is visible in the rising waters of the Pacific Ocean that recently prompted the prime minister of New Zealand to offer a haven to the residents of the island nation of Tuvalu as it slowly goes under. It is evident in the floods that, in 2002,

Rising water levels cause concern for low-lying cities such as Venice, where after one storm it was deep enough for kayakers to paddle in St. Mark's Square.

ANOTHER OPINION

Carbon Dioxide Traps Heat

"You don't have to consult a thermometer to see that the world is warming. Why is it happening? It cannot be explained by increases in the amount of sunlight reaching the Earth or a change in the planet's orbit, or by any other natural factors that influence major climatic events such as ice ages. But since industrial times there has been a 35 percent increase in concentrations of carbon dioxide in the atmosphere. Carbon dioxide traps heat. Hence, it is the most likely explanation we have for the rising temperature."

New Scientist, "It's All Around Us: Every Shred of Evidence Shows Global Warming Is Really Happening," March 18, 2006.

inundated whole cities in Germany, Russia, and the Czech Republic. It is underscored in the United States by the spread of West Nile virus to forty-two states—and to 230 species of birds, insects, and animals—and in the record-setting 412 tornadoes that leveled whole towns during a ten-day span in May 2003. Its reality is visible from outer space—where satellites have detected an increase in the radiation from greenhouse gases—to our own backyards.

Seen in its full dimensions, the challenge of global climate change seems truly overwhelming. In the absence of a compelling and obvious solution, the most natural human tendency is simply not to want to know about it.

When a crisis becomes so apparent that denial is no longer tenable, the typical response is to minimize the scope of the problem and embrace partial, inadequate solutions. Witness the voluntary approach of the Bush administration as well as the low goals of the Kyoto Protocol, which calls for industrial countries to cut their aggregate emissions by 5.2 percent below 1990 levels, by 2012. (The goal for the United States under the treaty was reductions of 7 percent below 1990 levels.)

Science Clearly Indicates a Crisis

By contrast, the science is unambiguous: To pacify our increasingly unstable climate requires humanity to cut its use of coal and oil by 70 percent in a very short time. The grudging response in the United States, and to a lesser extent, abroad, reflects more than a profound underestimation of the scope and urgency of the problem. It betrays an equivalent underestimation of the truly transformative potential of an appropriate solution. Given the scope of the challenge, a real solution to the climate crisis seems to offer a historically unique opportunity to begin to mend a profoundly fractured world.

But it all begins with the climate—and the stunningly rapid atmospheric buildup of carbon dioxide emissions from our fossil fuels. This is trapping growing amounts of heat inside our atmosphere, heat that has historically radiated back into space.

Unintentionally, we have set in motion massive systems of the planet (with huge amounts of inertia) that have kept it relatively hospitable to civilization for the last 10,000 years. With our burning of coal and oil, we have heated the deep oceans. We have reversed the carbon cycle by more than 400,000 years. We have loosed a wave of violent and chaotic weather. We have altered the timing of the seasons. We are living on an increasingly precarious margin of stability.

The accelerating rate of climate change is spelled out in two recent studies—one on the environmental side, one on the energy side.

The Hadley Study

In 2001, researchers at the Hadley Center, Britain's main climate research institute, found that the climate will change 50 percent more quickly than was previously assumed. That is because earlier computer models calculated the impacts of a warming atmosphere on a relatively static biosphere. But when they factored in the warming that has already taken place, they found that the rate of change is compounding. Their projections show that many of the world's forests will begin to turn from sinks (vegetation that absorbs carbon dioxide) to sources (vegetation that releases carbon dioxide)—dying off and emitting carbon—by around 2040.

The other study, from the energy side, is equally troubling. [In 2001] a team of researchers reported in the journal *Nature* that unless the world is getting half its energy from noncarbon sources by 2018, we will see an inevitable doubling—and possible tripling—of atmospheric carbon levels later in this century. In 2002, a follow-up study by many of the same researchers, published in the journal *Science*, called for a Manhattan-type crash project to develop renewable energy sources—wind, solar, and hydrogen fuel. Using conservative estimates of future

As Carbon Emissions Rise, So Do Global Temperatures

Temperature Increase

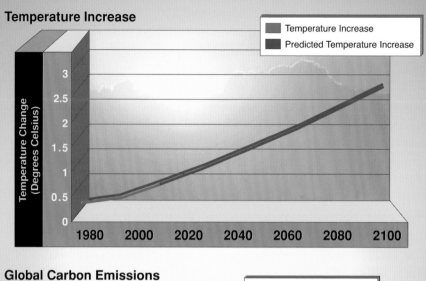

Legend:
- Temperature Increase
- Predicted Temperature Increase

Y-axis: Temperature Change (Degrees Celsius): 0, 0.5, 1, 1.5, 2, 2.5, 3

X-axis: 1980, 2000, 2020, 2040, 2060, 2080, 2100

Global Carbon Emissions

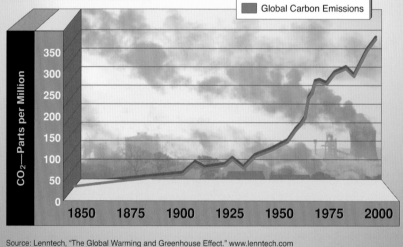

Legend:
- Global Carbon Emissions

Y-axis: CO_2—Parts per Million: 0, 50, 100, 150, 200, 250, 300, 350

X-axis: 1850, 1875, 1900, 1925, 1950, 1975, 2000

Source: Lenntech, "The Global Warming and Greenhouse Effect." www.lenntech.com

energy use, the researchers found that within fifty years, humanity must generate at least three times more energy from noncarbon sources than the world currently produces from fossil fuels to avoid a catastrophic buildup of atmospheric CO_2 later in this century.

For nearly a decade after it surfaced as a public issue in 1988, climate change was regarded primarily as a remote, almost futuristic, threat based on an arcane branch of science that depended on the mind-numbing complexity and paralyzing uncertainty of an early generation of computer models whose reliability was too suspect to justify enormous policy changes.

In 1995, the issue gained prominence when the world's community of climate scientists first declared they had detected the "human influence" on the climate. That finding legitimized global climate change as a major environmental issue. As a consequence, climate change was subsequently accorded the same mix of rhetorical concern and political inaction as most other environmental issues.

The Issue Is More Urgent than Ever

In 2001, however, the issue was infused with a jolt of urgency. That January, the U.N. Intergovernmental Panel on Climate Change (IPCC) concluded that the climate is changing far more rapidly than scientists had previously projected.

More than 2,000 scientists from 100 countries, participating in the largest and most rigorously peer-reviewed scientific collaboration in history, reported to the UN that brutal droughts, floods, and violent storms across the planet will intensify because emissions from humanity's burning of coal and oil is driving up temperatures much more rapidly than scientists had anticipated just six years earlier.

"The most comprehensive study on the subject [indicates] that Earth's average temperature could rise by as much as 10.4 degrees over the next 100 years—the most rapid change in 10 millennia and more than 60 percent higher than the same group predicted less than six years ago," according to the *Washington Post*.

The Impact of Climate Change

Rising temperatures will melt ice sheets and raise sea levels by as much as thirty-four inches, causing floods that could displace tens of millions of people in low-lying areas—such as China's Pearl River Delta, much of Bangladesh, and the most densely populated area of Egypt.

Droughts will parch farmlands and aggravate world hunger. Storms triggered by such climatic extremes as El Niño will become more frequent. Diseases such as malaria and dengue fever will spread, the report noted.

A second working group of the IPCC—one that focused on the impacts of coming climate changes—reached the extremely sobering conclusion that "most of earth's inhabitants will be losers," in the words of the group's co-chair, James McCarthy of Harvard University.

The report concluded that poor countries in Africa, Asia, and Latin America with limited resources would bear the brunt of the most extreme climate changes. It added that economic losses from natural catastrophes increased from about $4 billion a year in the 1950s to $40 billion in 1999, with about one-fourth of the losses occurring in developing countries.

(Two years later, nature had already upped the ante. In 2003, the United Nations reported that climate impacts cost the world $60 billion that year, an increase of 10 percent over the $55 billion in climate-related damages in 2002.)

"The scientific consensus presented in this comprehensive report about human-induced climate change should sound alarm bells in every national capital and in every local community. We should start preparing ourselves," declared Klaus Topfer, director of the United Nations Environment Programme (UNEP).

In the fall of 2003, a succession of events—climatic, economic, and political—coalesced into a vivid mosaic that reflects the reach and variety of climate impacts and their reverberation through our economic and political institutions.

Ominous Findings

Several developments . . . were particularly ominous because of their scope:

- The entire ecosystem of the North Sea was found to be in a state of collapse because of rising water temperatures.

- For the first time in recorded history, the world consumed more grain than it produced for *four years in a row*. The reason: rising temperatures and falling water tables—both consequences of global climate change.

- The German government declared that the goals of the Kyoto Protocol need to be increased by a factor of four to avoid "catastrophic" changes. Otherwise, the climate will change at a rate not seen in the last million years.

- The most highly publicized impact of global warming in 2003 involved a succession of headlines from Europe about an extraordinary summertime heat wave. Scientists attributed the unusually high mortality rates not to the fact that the August temperatures were so much higher than before. The record-setting temperatures provided only a partial explanation. The link between climate change and the deaths of so many Europeans had been established in a laboratory of the U.S. National Oceanic and Atmospheric Administration (NOAA) nearly six years earlier, when researchers at NOAA's National Climatic Data Center found that, as Earth's temperature has been rising, the nighttime low temperatures have been rising nearly twice as fast as the daytime high temperatures. Before the buildup

Parisians cool off in a public fountain during a record heat wave. Such heat waves are thought to be one indication of global warming.

of heat-trapping carbon dioxide in the atmosphere, daytime and nighttime temperatures generally rose and fell in parallel. But as carbon levels in the atmosphere have thickened, they have tended to trap heat during the evenings, preventing it from radiating back into space once the sun has faded into the nighttime sky.

- In August 2003, that finding took on an especially grisly reality. The lingering nighttime warmth in Europe that summer deprived overheated Europeans of the normal relief from blistering daytime temperatures. As a result, people were not able to recuperate from the heat stress they had suffered during the relentlessly hot days. When that brutal summer finally subsided, it left more than 35,000 people dead.

- The following month, silently and out of view of most of the world, the biggest ice sheet in the Arctic—3,000 years old, 80 feet thick, and 150 square miles in area—collapsed from warming surface waters in September 2003. The Ward Hunt Ice Shelf, located 500 miles from the North Pole on the edge of Canada's Ellesmere Island, broke in two. A massive freshwater lake long held back by the ice also drained away.

- The same month brought another startling—and largely unanticipated—consequence of our fossil fuel use. Scientists reported that the pH level of the world's oceans had changed more in the last 100 years than it had in the previous 10,000 years—primarily because of the fallout from emissions caused by coal and oil burning. In short, the oceans are becoming acidified.

- By the fall of 2003, an eighteen-month drought in Australia had cut farm incomes in half—and left many scientists speculating that the prolonged drought may have become a permanent condition in one of the country's richest food-growing areas. . . .

Hope for a Better Climate Future

But the real news about climate change is not about its destructive potential. The real news lies in the extraordinary opportu-

A scuba diver monitors a rig that collects oil from deep under the ocean. Such drilling techniques can cause environmental harm.

nity the climate crisis presents to us. Given how very central energy is to our existence, a solution to climate change—which is appropriate to the magnitude of the problem—could also begin to reverse some very discouraging and destructive political and economic dynamics as well.

Nature's requirement that humanity cut its use of carbon fuels by 70 percent in a very short time leaves us with basically two choices. We can either regress into a far more primitive and energy-poor lifestyle—or we can mount a global project to replace every oil-burning furnace, every coal-fired generating plant, and every gasoline-burning car with noncarbon and renewable energy sources. A properly framed plan to rewire the globe with solar energy, hydrogen fuel cells, wind farms, and

Clean, renewable solar power is collected from rooftop panels. It is hoped that solar and other alternative energies will provide viable alternatives to oil.

other sources of clean energy would do much more than stave off the most disruptive manifestations of climate change. Depending on how it is structured, a global transition to renewable energy could create huge numbers of new jobs, especially in developing countries. It could turn dependent and impoverished countries into robust trading partners. It could significantly expand the overall wealth in the global economy. It could provide many of the earth's most deprived inhabitants with a sense of personal future and individual purpose.

The Seeds for Real Security

That same solution also contains the seeds for real security in a world that threatens to become polarized between totalitarians and terrorists.

It could very well trigger a major change in many unsustainable practices that are threatening many other natural systems—the world's forests and oceans, for example—whose vitality is already at risk.

It could be the prompt that reverses the kind of exaggerated nationalism that threatens to re-tribalize humanity. Rather than hastening our regression into a more splintered, combative, and degraded world, it could be the springboard that propels us forward into a much more cooperative and coordinated global community.

The same solution to the climate crisis could also begin to put people in charge of governments and governments in charge of corporations. A program to rewire the world with clean energy could provide the outlines of a model in which people would put democratically determined boundaries around the operations of multinational corporations.

In the long run, the solutions to the climate crisis could establish equity as a universal human value and resuscitate participatory democracy as a governing operating principle that reorganizes our relationships to each other, to other nations, to the global economy, and most fundamentally, to the planet on which we all depend.

In this immense drama of uncertain outcome, this much is true: A major discontinuity is inevitable. The collective life we have lived as a species for thousands of years will not continue long into the future. We will either see the fabric of civilization unravel under the onslaught of an increasingly unstable climate—or else we will use the construction of a new global energy infrastructure to begin to forge a new set of global relationships.

If we are truly lucky—and visionary enough—those new relationships will differ dramatically from what we have known throughout our recorded history. They will be based far less on what divides us as a species and far more on what unites us. Embedded in the gathering fury of nature is a hidden gift—an opportunity to begin to redeem an increasingly fragmented world.

The alternative is a certain and rapid descent into climate hell.

The Link Between Oil Use and Global Warming Is a Myth

David Bellamy

Professor and environmentalist David Bellamy argues that the theory of global warming is a myth. Bellamy believes that rises in Earth's temperature are part of the planet's normal climate cycle. Moreover, he argues, carbon dioxide in the atmosphere is actually good for plants. Bellamy expresses concern that the fear of global warming will result in the waste of billions of dollars as governments attempt to address a problem that does not exist.

Whatever the experts say about the howling gales, thunder and lightning we've had over the past two days, of one thing we can be certain. Someone, somewhere—and there is every chance it will be a politician or an environmentalist—will blame the weather on global warming.

But they will be 100 per cent wrong. Global warming—at least the modern nightmare version—is a myth. I am sure of it and so are a growing number of scientists. But what is really worrying is that the world's politicians and policy makers are not.

Instead, they have an unshakeable belief in what has, unfortunately, become one of the central credos of the environmental movement. Humans burn fossil fuels, which release increased levels of carbon dioxide—the principal so-called greenhouse gas—into the atmosphere, causing the atmosphere to heat up.

David Bellamy, "Global Warming? What a Load of Poppycock!" *Daily Mail*, 2004. Reproduced by permission of the author.

They say this is global warming: I say this is poppycock. Unfortunately, for the time being, it is their view that prevails.

As a result of their ignorance, the world's economy may be about to divert billions, nay trillions of pounds, dollars and roubles into solving a problem that actually doesn't exist. The waste of economic resources is incalculable and tragic.

Carbon Dioxide Is Not Bad for the Planet

To explain why I believe that global warming is largely a natural phenomenon that has been with us for 13,000 years and probably isn't causing us any harm anyway, we need to take heed of some basic facts of botanical science.

For a start, carbon dioxide is *not* the dreaded killer greenhouse gas that the 1992 Earth Summit in Rio de Janeiro and the subsequent Kyoto Protocol [to reduce greenhouse gas emissions] five years later cracked it up to be. It is, in fact, the most important airborne fertiliser in the world, and without it there would be no green plants at all.

That is because, as any schoolchild will tell you, plants take in carbon dioxide and water and, with the help of a little sunshine, convert them into complex carbon compounds—that we either eat, build with or just admire—and oxygen, which just happens to keep the rest of the planet alive.

Increase the amount of carbon dioxide in the atmosphere, double it even, and this would produce a rise in plant productivity. Call me a biased old plant lover but that doesn't sound like much of a killer gas to me. Hooray for global warming is what I say, and so do a lot of my fellow scientists.

Other Scientists Agree

Let me quote from a petition produced by the Oregon Institute of Science and Medicine, which has been signed by over 18,000 scientists who are totally opposed to the Kyoto Protocol, which committed the world's leading industrial nations to cut their production of greenhouse gasses from fossil fuels.

They say: 'Predictions of harmful climatic effects due to future increases in minor greenhouse gasses like carbon dioxide are in error and do not conform to experimental knowledge.'

Some experts suggest that carbon dioxide, a byproduct of burning fossil fuels, does not harm the environment, but instead helps plants grow.

You couldn't get much plainer than that. And yet we still have public figures such as Sir David King, scientific adviser to Her Majesty's Government [in Great Britain], making preposterous statements such as 'by the end of this century, the only continent we will be able to live on is Antarctica.'

At the same time, he's joined the bandwagon that blames just about everything on global warming, regardless of the scientific evidence. For example, take the alarm about rising sea levels around the south coast of England and subsequent flooding along the region's rivers. According to Sir David, global warming is largely to blame.

But it isn't at all—it's down to bad management of water catchments, building on flood plains and the incontestable fact that the south of England is gradually sinking below the waves.

And that sinking is nothing to do with rising sea levels caused by ice-caps melting. Instead, it is purely related to an entirely natural warping of the Earth's crust, which could only be reversed by sticking one of the enormously heavy ice-caps from past ice ages back on top of Scotland.

Increased flooding can be blamed on bad management of water catchments and poor city design rather than global warming, according to some experts.

Ah, ice ages . . . those absolutely massive changes in global climate that environmentalists don't like to talk about because they provide such strong evidence that climate change is an entirely natural phenomenon.

It was round about the end of the last ice age, some 13,000 years ago, that a global warming process did undoubtedly begin.

Not because of all those Stone age folk roasting mammoth meat on fossil fuel camp fires but because of something called the 'Milankovitch Cycles,' an entirely natural fact of planetary life that depends on the tilt of the Earth's axis and its orbit around the sun.

Natural Climate Cycles Occur

The glaciers melted, the ice cap retreated and Stone Age man could begin hunting again. But a couple of millennia later, it got very cold again and everyone headed south. Then it warmed up so much that water from melted ice filled the English Channel and we became an island.

The truth is that the climate has been yo-yo-ing up and down ever since. Whereas it was warm enough for Romans to produce good wine in York, on the other hand, King Canute had to dig up peat to warm his people. And then it started getting warm again.

Up and down, up and down—that is how temperature and climate have always gone in the past and there is no proof they are not still doing exactly the same thing now. In other words, climate change is an entirely natural phenomenon, nothing to do with the burning of fossil fuels.

In fact, a recent scientific paper, rather unenticingly titled 'Atmospheric Carbon Dioxide Concentrations Over The Last Glacial Termination,' proved it.

It showed that increases in temperature are responsible for increases in atmospheric carbon dioxide levels, not the other way around.

The Global Warming Panic Is Costly

But this sort of evidence is ignored, either by those who believe the Kyoto Protocol is environmental gospel or by those who know 25 years of hard work went into securing the agreement and simply can't admit that the science it is based on is wrong.

Solar Activity, Not Carbon Dioxide, Warms the Earth

It's Solar Activity...

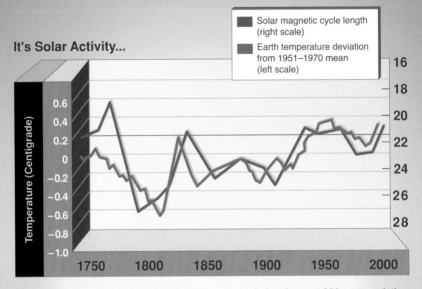

The graph above shows deviations in temperatures during the past 250 years, relative to the mean temperature from 1951 to 1970. It also shows the length of the solar cycle during this period. The shorter the solar cycle, the more active, and therefore brighter, the sun. The close correlation between these two measures demonstrates that changes in the sun's brightness can account for global warming.

... Not Carbon Dioxide

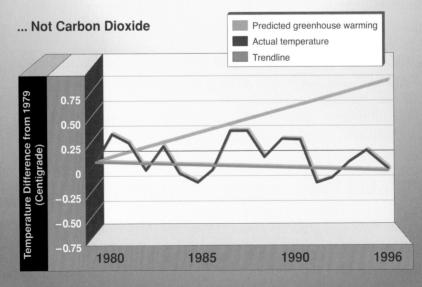

Source: Arthur B. Robinson and Zachary W. Robinson, *The Wall Street Journal*, December 4, 1997.

The real truth is that the main greenhouse gas—the one that has the most direct effect on land temperature—is water vapour, 99 per cent of which is entirely natural.

If all the water vapour was removed from the atmosphere, the temperature would fall by 33 degrees Celsius. But, remove all the carbon dioxide and the temperature might fall by just 0.3 per cent.

Although we wouldn't be around, because without it there would be no green plants, no herbivorous farm animals and no food for us to eat.

It has been estimated that the cost of cutting fossil fuel emissions in line with the Kyoto Protocol would be £76 trillion. Little wonder, then, that world leaders are worried. So should we all be.

If we signed up to these scaremongers, we could be about to waste a gargantuan amount of money on a problem that doesn't exist—money that could be used in umpteen better ways: fighting world hunger, providing clean water, developing alternative energy sources, improving our environment, creating jobs.

The link between the burning of fossil fuels and global warming is a myth. It is time the world's leaders, their scientific advisers and many environmental pressure groups woke up to the fact.

Oil Drilling Should Be Allowed in the Arctic National Wildlife Refuge

3

Arctic Power

The following article is a statement from Arctic Power, a nonprofit organization consisting of over ten thousand members who support drilling for oil in the Arctic National Wildlife Refuge in Alaska. The organization contends that oil drilling must be allowed in ANWR in order to reduce America's reliance on foreign oil. The organization also argues that ANWR is likely to contain a significant amount of oil, making it imperative that drilling start as soon as possible. Moreover, it maintains, drilling will not harm the environment, as has been proven by drilling in nearby Prudhoe Bay.

Less than 60 miles west of the border of ANWR lies Prudhoe Bay, North America's largest oil field. Prudhoe, together with the satellite fields of Kuparuk, Lisburne, Northstar, Endicott and Badami, currently account for about 16% of US domestic oil production. This is down from 25% of US production 15 years ago which made Prudhoe Bay the largest oil field in North American history.

Due to the fragile Arctic ecosystem Congress, along with the State of Alaska, and the Native Alaskan landholders required that extreme caution and measures be taken by the oil industry to develop Prudhoe Bay. Over the past 25 years millions of dollars of research on Arctic wildlife and their habitat, funded by oil royalties, have immeasurably increased the scientific understanding of the Arctic ecosystem. Indeed, the environmental requirements demanded in America, and the controversy over future ANWR development, have made this corner of the Arctic one of the most scientifically studied areas on the continent.

Oil Production Does Not Threaten Wildlife

Each year thousands of waterfowl and other birds nest and reproduce in the Prudhoe Bay oil fields and a healthy and increasing mammal population, including the 32,000 strong Central Caribou Herd, migrate through this area to give birth and feed. Oil field facilities have been designed to accommodate wildlife and utilize the least amount of tundra surface. All buildings are

Bears are among the hundreds of animal species that live undisturbed around the Trans-Alaska pipeline and other oil industry sites.

elevated and built on gravel pads to keep the tundra from thawing. All pipelines are elevated to allow caribou and animals to pass, and all structures including roads are planned and designed to pose minimal hindrance to wildlife movements.

In the past 30 years much has changed technologically as well. Drilling pad size has decreased from an average 140 acres down to 5 acres, while future new facilities will sit on cooled stilts without need for gravel pads. Drilling rigs can drill 8 miles horizontally now compared to 2 miles before. Drill pipes can also now branch out with feeder pipes called "multi-lateral drilling" requiring fewer wells drilled and thus a smaller footprint made. Ice roads connect "island" satellite facilities requiring no gravel roads, further minimizing environmental impact. Regulatory framework and permitting processes at the federal,

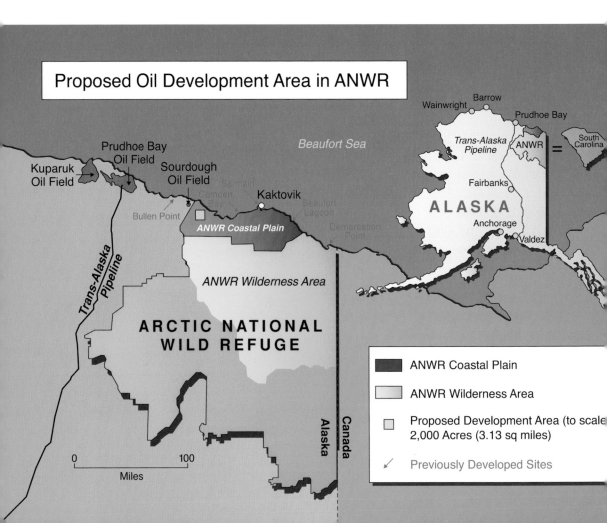

Proposed Oil Development Area in ANWR

state, and local (North Slope Borough) level require thoroughly researched and planned development activities focused foremost on environmental protection. All these activities are monitored by the US Environmental Protection Agency, and Fish and Game Departments daily.

High Petroleum Potential

Less than 5 miles from the satellite Badami field east of Prudhoe Bay lies the 10-02 Area of ANWR known as the Coastal Plain. It is flat, featureless, and treeless; geologically and ecologically, much the same as Prudhoe Bay. In 1998 the US Geological Survey issued a survey of the 10-02 Area and from this survey and others previous, the consensus of the geologic community is that the Coastal Plain of ANWR has the greatest onshore petroleum potential yet to be discovered in North America. This potential is believed to be on the order of 6-16 billions of barrels of recoverable oil and may rival that of the Prudhoe Bay field. However, should leasing be permitted and subsequent commercial discoveries be made, it will be an estimated 6-10 years before oil and gas production from ANWR reaches market. That production will then be urgently required by the United States.

Domestic Oil Production

Domestic crude oil production in the US has already declined from nearly 9 million barrels per day in 1985, to about 5 million barrels per day in 2006 leaving us in need to import over 60% of our oil supply. Even with only a modest 1–2% yearly growth in U.S. crude oil demand, the deficit in U.S. supplies will require millions of barrels per day to be obtained, and this oil will have to come from

> **ANOTHER OPINION** ➤
>
> ### ANWR Resources Can Be Extracted Safely
>
> "I fully understand the fears of many people that the presence of the oil industry on the coastal plains will disrupt the wildlife. . . . In 1969, when oil was first discovered on our [Inupiat] lands, those fears were foremost in our minds as we fought for self-determination in order to be able to protect our resources. Since then, we have had over twenty years of working with the oil industry here. We enacted strict regulations to protect our land and the oil companies have consistently met the standards we imposed. ANWR holds resources that can be extracted safely with care and concern for the entire eco-system it encompasses."
>
> Benjamin P. Nageak, "Inupiat Eskimos First, Best Environmentalists," www.anwr.org.

somewhere. The best, most promising place to look in North America is the 10-02 Area of ANWR. ANWR's contribution will therefore be critical to national energy needs.

Development in ANWR will keep our money at home, and mean we as a nation have greater control over our economy and security. Our national debt will decrease as will our dependence on many often not so friendly nations. ANWR oil will also create hundreds of thousands of domestic jobs in support industries such as ship building for tankers and steel pipes and facility construction, maintenance and supply. ANWR development will actually help the world environment too as Alaskan oil is the most environmentally carefully produced oil in the world and it will decrease our reliance on oil fields in countries that have no environmental regulations.

It is argued that drilling in the Arctic National Wildlife Refuge can help the economy by creating more oil industry jobs for Americans.

The issue of oil and gas leasing in the 8 percent of ANWR represented by the Coastal Plain should not be considered, therefore, as an "either/or" decision with respect to wildlife protection or development. The record of Prudhoe Bay over the last 30 years supports and proves the success of multiple use management concepts in the Arctic. Nevertheless, in issuing its decision with regard to future management of the Coastal Plain of the Arctic National Wildlife Refuge, Congress will be faced with the challenge of reconciling diverse goals, national needs for additional domestic energy supplies, the national need and interest in preservation of wilderness, and the promise (in ANCSA and ANILCA) to Alaska Natives regarding continued availability of subsistence fish and wildlife resources on their private lands. These goals are not, however, mutually exclusive. Given the oil and gas exploration and production technology existing today and particularly the support of the Natives who live in ANWR, and whom are the real caretakers of the land, the ANWR Coastal Plain can be opened to leasing that is consistent with all of these important requirements.

4 Oil Drilling Should Not Be Allowed in the Arctic National Wildlife Refuge

Natural Resources Defense Council

In the following selection, members of the Natural Resources Defense Council (NRDC), a national environmental action organization, argue against drilling for oil in the Arctic National Wildlife Refuge in Alaska. The NRDC points out that the majority of Americans are against drilling for oil in ANWR. The organization also asserts that recent efforts to win approval for drilling are motivated by bigger profits for oil companies, not energy independence. In fact, according to the NRDC, there is only enough oil in the ANWR to supply America with oil for one year. The NRDC believes that drilling would destroy the fragile tundra environment.

On the northern edge of our continent, stretching from the peaks of the Brooks Range across a vast expanse of tundra to the Beaufort Sea, lies Alaska's Arctic National Wildlife Refuge. An American Serengeti, the Arctic Refuge continues to pulse with million-year-old ecological rhythms. It is the greatest living reminder that conserving nature in its wild state is a core American value. . . .

"Arctic National Wildlife Refuge: A Wilderness Worth Far More than Oil,"
http://www.nrdc.org/land/wilderness/arctic.asp, 2005. Reproduced with permission from the Natural Resources Defense Council.

Americans Have Steadily Opposed Drilling in the Arctic Refuge

The controversy over drilling in the Arctic Refuge—the last piece of America's Arctic coastline not already open to oil exploration—isn't new. Big Oil has long sought access to the refuge's coastal plain, a fragile swath of tundra that teems with staggering numbers of birds and animals. During the [George W.] Bush administration's first term, repeated attempts were made to open the refuge. But time after time, the American public rejected the idea. Congress has received hundreds of thousands of emails, faxes and phone calls from citizens opposed to drilling in the Arctic Refuge, an outpouring that has helped make the difference. And polls have consistently shown that a solid majority of Americans oppose drilling; a December 2004 Zogby Survey found that 55 percent of respondents oppose drilling, and that 59 percent consider attaching this issue to the budget process to be a "backdoor maneuver."

Drilling in the Arctic National Wildlife Refuge could displace buffalo and the 200 other species of animals that make their home in the region.

Despite repeated failure and stiff opposition, drilling proponents press on. Why? Remarks from [former] House majority leader Tom DeLay, in a closed-door session of House GOP [Republican] leadership, reveal the true agenda. "It's about precedent," said DeLay. He believes that opening the Arctic Refuge will turn the corner in the broader national debate over whether or not energy, timber, mining and other industries should be allowed into pristine wild areas across the country. Next up: Greater Yellowstone? Our western canyonlands? Our coastal waters?

The drive to drill the Arctic Refuge is about oil company profits and lifting barriers to future exploration in protected lands, pure and simple. It has nothing to do with energy independence. Opening the Arctic Refuge to energy development is about transferring our public estate into corporate hands, so it can be liquidated for a quick buck.

Arctic Refuge Oil Is a Distraction, Not a Solution

What would America gain by allowing heavy industry into the refuge? Very little. Oil from the refuge would hardly make a dent in our dependence on foreign imports—leaving our economy and way of life just as exposed to wild swings in worldwide oil prices and supply as it is today. The truth is, we simply can't drill our way to energy independence.

Although drilling proponents often say there are 16 billion barrels of oil under the refuge's coastal plain, the U.S. Geological Service's estimate of the amount that could be recovered economically—that is, the amount likely to be profitably extracted and sold—represents less than a year's U.S. supply.

It would take 10 years for any Arctic Refuge oil to reach the market, and even when production peaks—in the distant year of 2027—the refuge would produce a paltry 1 or 2 percent of Americans' daily consumption. Whatever oil the refuge might produce is simply irrelevant to the larger issue of meeting America's future energy needs.

Giving Future Generations a Pristine Arctic

Oil produced from the Arctic Refuge would come at enormous, and irreversible, cost. The refuge is among the world's last true wildernesses, and it is one of the largest sanctuaries for Arctic animals. Traversed by a dozen rivers and framed by jagged peaks, this spectacular wilderness is a vital birthing

Environmentalists worry that caribou (left) and polar bear populations would be endangered if drilling were to occur in their birthing grounds.

An oil worker cleans up after an oil spill in Prudhoe Bay. Such spills can cause irreparable damage to the environment.

ground for polar bears, grizzlies, Arctic wolves, caribou and the endangered shaggy musk ox, a mammoth-like survivor of the last Ice Age.

For a sense of what big oil's heavy machinery would do to the refuge, just look 60 miles west to Prudhoe Bay—a gargantuan oil complex that has turned 1,000 square miles of fragile tundra into a sprawling industrial zone containing 1,500 miles of roads and pipelines, 1,400 producing wells and three jetports. The result is a landscape defaced by mountains of sewage sludge, scrap metal, garbage and more than 60 contaminated waste sites that contain—and often leak—acids, lead, pesticides, solvents and diesel fuel.

While proponents of drilling insist the Arctic Refuge could be developed by disturbing as little as 2,000 acres within the 1.5-million-acre coastal plain, a recent analysis by NRDC [the Natural Resources Defense Council] reveals this to be pure myth. Why? Because U.S. Geological Survey studies have found that oil in the refuge isn't concentrated in a single, large reservoir. Rather, it's spread across the coastal plain in more than 30 small deposits, which would require vast networks of roads and pipelines that would fragment the habitat, disturbing and displacing wildlife.

A Responsible Path to Energy Security

The solution to America's energy problems will be found in American ingenuity, not more oil. Only by reducing our reliance on oil—foreign and domestic—and investing in cleaner, renewable forms of power will our country achieve true energy security. The good news is that we already have many of the tools we need to accomplish this. For example, Detroit has the technology right now to produce high-performance hybrid cars, trucks and SUVs; if America made the transition to these more efficient vehicles, far more oil would be saved than the Arctic Refuge is likely to produce. Doesn't that make far more sense than selling out our natural heritage and exploiting one of our true wilderness gems?

Oil Spills Are a Serious Problem

Page Spencer

The following article is excerpted from the journal of Page Spencer, an ecologist with the National Park Service and a native Alaskan. When the *Exxon Valdez* oil tanker spilled millions of gallons of crude oil into Prince William Sound in Alaska in 1989, Spencer was called in by the National Parks Service to monitor the effects of the spill on the environment. Thousands of animals perished immediately after the oil spill, and scientists continue to study the impact of the spill on the Alaskan environment. Spencer's writing reveals the devastation caused by the largest oil spill in the history of the United States. She describes the overpowering smell of the oil, her glimpse of dying seabirds, and the grief she feels over the destruction she witnesses.

We're up early in the grey light. From the pilot house, I watch the radar scope and rock walls as Eric [Olson, our crew member] maneuvers *Shaman* [the rented boat] out of Taz Basin [in Alaska]. Rocks close in almost to touching as the bottom rises to a lip on the fathometer. Then *Shaman* brushes over the kelp and out into the gentle swells on the west side of Granite Island. We cruise on down the island, around Granite Cape, and weave our way east through the islands to the Chiswells.

The First Encounter with the Oil Spill

Here I encounter the oil slick first hand. After all the sampling and testing and wondering what it will be like, there is no doubt. The smell is nearly overpowering. The oil lays on the water surface as a blue-grey coverlet. The surface wind ruffling is dampened. At the edges, the thinner oil gleams in iridescent colors: yellows, blues, green, red. Thick brown globs float in the slick, the leading edge of obscene diarrhea from a sick monster. Only a few sea lions remain on the haulout rocks where we saw hundreds just three days ago. I finally spot about 50 swimming in the slick just off the rocks. Kittiwakes and gulls swirl overhead. Although the air resounds with gull screams and sea lion grunts, there seems to be a deathly stillness in the place.

Soberly, we go about the business of taking notes and collecting samples. Somehow we make the problem smaller by focusing on the scientific tasks. Oil is reduced when it is in a 125 ml jar. The globs are like heavy bearing grease, and Randy

A sea lion's fur is stained with oil following an oil spill. Oil spills can have devastating consequences for marine creatures.

[Upton, our crewmember] only gets it off his hands after scrubbing vigorously with Simple Green cleaner. Silently, we leave this place and head northeast.

The oil coverage is in large patches. About one mile off Pilot Rock we encounter another wide band of oil and are still in it when we reach Barwell Island. Off the south side of Rugged Island we watch five whales spouting and swimming in the slick. It doesn't seem to quite touch the shore, holding just back of the line of breakers on the rocks. As we approach Barwell Island the oil is thick and stretches south as far as we can see.

Large flocks of kittiwakes and gulls wheel overhead, and kittiwakes and murres are rafted on the water in the oil. This is the beginning of migration arrival for many seabirds. Exhausted from the long flights, they raft up to rest and feed for awhile before beginning the arduous work of nesting and raising young. The rocky islands and headlands of this coast are some of the prime nesting habitat in the world for these species. In the weeks ahead, hundreds of thousands of birds will arrive to stay or pass through to other nesting areas. As they dive to feed and surface to raft with their companions, it is incomprehensible that they will not be contaminated sooner or later. External oil becomes internal toxins when the birds preen, trying to restore loft to sticky feathers. As the *Shaman* approaches the island we see birds with dark patches in white feathers.

The Oil Is Everywhere

The oil lies thick around Barwell Island, right up to the steep rock walls. The swells slosh gently forward and slurp back, continually washing the shore with oily water. The smell of petroleum is very strong, completely overpowering the normal sea smells of salt air and clean kelp. I ask Eric to go through the pass

Birds covered in oil will ingest the toxic substance when they attempt to preen their feathers.

between Barwell Island and the cape. The oil has pooled here, an inch thick or more. We see more and more birds with oiled feathers, and I realize that we can't tell where oil ends and black feathers begin. Bobbing in the pass, we collect samples, take photos, notes. The rocks near the sea are sloping on the back side of the island. As I stand on the bow I notice movement in the dark rocks. Looking closer, I see a murre right at the water's edge, being washed by every breaking wave. She is completely black, her normal white breast feathers covered with oil. As each wave washes her anew with oil, she staggers to keep balance. Her wings flap feebly but don't generate any lift to fly. She tries to hop up the rock surface to escape the waves, but slides back down in the oil. The only part that seems to work is her tail, which she shakes vigorously after every wave.

As I stand alone on the bow, a deep grief begins to emerge in me. Beginning in my belly, it rises through my being and surfaces as sobs which shake my soul. The enormity of the horror washes

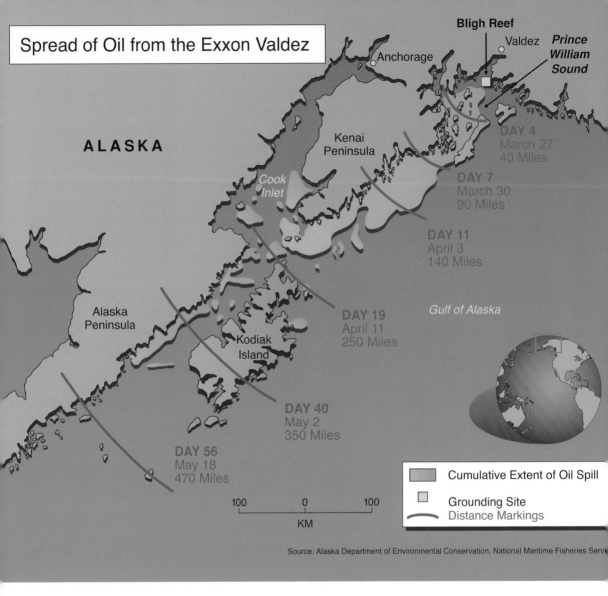

Spread of Oil from the Exxon Valdez

Bligh Reef

Valdez

Prince William Sound

Anchorage

Kenai Peninsula

ALASKA

Cook Inlet

DAY 4
March 27
40 Miles

DAY 7
March 30
90 Miles

DAY 11
April 3
140 Miles

Gulf of Alaska

Alaska Peninsula

Kodiak Island

DAY 19
April 11
250 Miles

DAY 40
May 2
350 Miles

DAY 56
May 18
470 Miles

100   0   100

KM

Cumulative Extent of Oil Spill

Grounding Site
Distance Markings

Source: Alaska Department of Environmental Conservation, National Maritime Fisheries Servi

over me, watching this lone bird beginning to die, struggling to live, in the stench of gasoline. The ecologist in me has known for days the destruction the oil is causing to entire ecosystems. Not just the death of individual animals, plants, plankton and lifestyles; but the total changes in the energy flow through the system. The dynamic flow of energy, nutrients and life is altered, blocked. The functioning chain of life, ebbing and flowing from one organism to another, from one generation to the next, no longer functions. The processes which flow through the land also flow through my being, and I feel the lurching, the recoiling, the aberrations in the smoothly functioning system. Tears overflow and course down my face, dropping onto the deck at my feet. A commotion at the stern brushes forward. "A bird, a dead bird." Someone rushes up to me: "Should we get it? Do we need it for a specimen?" Mutely I nod my head and stumble into the pilot house. Eric sees my tears and holds me tightly. "No need to apologize," he says, "I feel the same way." Gradually my sobs subside and settle over my heart like a heavy wet blanket. Quietly, *Shaman* powers up again and we head up Resurrection Bay. The oil only goes up the bay a short ways, and soon we are out of it.

Taking Action to Clean Up the Spill

We swing into Thumb Cove. Bright orange curtain boom is stretched across the creek mouth. It stands tall and garish against the tree and mountain pattern reflected in the calm sea. The people of Seward have not waited for EXXON to bring equipment and supplies to protect their salmon fisheries. Calls

It can take years to undo the damage inflicted by oil spills on the environment.

in the night and old contacts bring a planeload of scarce boom, and it is deployed by local boats just ahead of the oil coming across the Gulf. . . .

The dock is crowded as Eric berths *Shaman*. Anne Castellina, the Superintendent of the park, meets me with a big hug, and our closeknit crew is inundated by park people and press. . . . I am the last of the scientists off, loaded down with my equipment, and most of the people have dispersed. A lone photographer catches me as I come wearily down the dock. Up at the park office, people and questions swirl about in confusion. We bring the first oil samples from outside Prince William Sound. During the four days we were gone, an army of people has descended on Seward, focused on the park and the information we bring back.

Oil Spills Are Rare

Battelle Environmental Updates

The following selection originally appeared in the Summer 2001 edition of *Battelle Environmental Updates*, the official newsletter of Battelle, a global science and technology company. Battelle argues that large marine oil spills such as the 1989 *Exxon Valdez* spill in Prince William Sound, Alaska, are rare. When such a spill does occur, the company contends, cleanup is immediate and extensive. Battelle scientists have concluded that areas affected by oil spills recover in a matter of years.

Despite perceptions to the contrary, oil tanker accidents resulting in large marine oil spills are rare. When a large oil spill does occur in coastal waters, however, the immediate injury to marine ecosystems can in some cases be massive, especially if the oil washes ashore. Plants and animals living in the intertidal zone, as well as animals that use the sea surface, are the most vulnerable to spill injury, and large numbers can be killed in a short time.

Though oiled shorelines require cleanup, cleanup can cause harm to shoreline communities in addition to that caused by the oil itself. Thus, there is a strong need to answer the question, "how clean is clean?" How much oil should be removed to allow recovery to occur while minimizing additional harm from cleanup activities? Within a few days of the *Exxon Valdez* oil spill in March 1989 in Prince William Sound, Alaska, Exxon requested the help of senior Battelle scientists to answer these questions and to help determine the effects of the spill and the progress of ecosystem recovery following the spill.

Battelle Environmental Updates, "Ecosystem Recovery from Oil Spills—How Clean Is Clean?" *Battelle Environmental Updates*, 2001. Reproduced by permission.

An oil worker cleans rocks affected by an oil spill. Though devastating, oil spills are relatively rare.

Cleanup Is Thorough

The *Exxon Valdez* oil spill is the most contentious and extensively studied spill in history. Although the spill was smaller than many, it occurred in an area of high marine productivity and diversity. Exxon assumed responsibility for the cleanup and, in collaboration with the U.S. Coast Guard, mounted the largest oil spill cleanup in history.

The cleanup efforts supplemented by the scouring activity of severe winter storms removed most of the oil from the shore within one year of the spill. By 1992, the Coast Guard declared the Sound clean. Disagreement persists today as to the magnitude of the harm caused by the spill to marine ecosystems and the extent of ecosystem recovery.

There has been considerable disagreement between the trustees and Exxon-sponsored scientists concerning the impacts on commercial fishery species and shoreline communities. Studies performed by Battelle's Dr. Jerry Neff showed that concentrations of petroleum hydrocarbons in the water column never reached high enough concentrations to harm pelagic fish. Additionally, Battelle's Dr. Walter Pearson and colleagues showed that very little of the shoreline where herring deposited their eggs ever became oiled. Commercial catches of pink salmon and herring were at record highs for several years after the spill, indicating minimal harm to these populations.

Disagreements Over the Effectiveness of Cleanup

Many scientists assumed that the Sound was essentially pristine before the spill and that any evidence of petroleum hydrocarbons in the environment or changes in biological communities could be attributed to the spill. Detective work by Battelle's

An otter swims in Prince William sound. Though the Sound was the site of the Exxon Valdez oil spill, wildlife now thrive there.

Dr. Paul Boehm and Dr. Gregory Douglas used advanced oil fingerprinting methods to show that there were and still are many other sources of petroleum hydrocarbons in the Sound. In fact, much of the hydrocarbons in offshore sediments were determined to be not from the spill, but instead from eroding shales and related natural oil seeps along the coast southeast of the Sound. Additional work showed that hydrocarbons in some western areas of the Sound were derived from earlier human activities.

Small amounts of oil from the *Exxon Valdez* can still be found in the Sound; most is present in the upper intertidal "splash zone" of rocky shores and has the appearance of hard asphalt. Some oil is buried deep in the sediments, removed from the environment. The weathered oil to which animals may be exposed is in a location and physical form that is not harmful to marine plants and animals living in the intertidal zone. Several shoreline studies performed by Dr. Paul Boehm and colleagues on ecological effects of the oil and recovery of oiled shorelines have shown that the formerly oiled shorelines recovered within two to four years after the spill.

Toxicity tests on shoreline sediments with a common shoreline crustacean, conducted as part of the well-established sediment quality "triad" approach (chemistry, toxicology, ecology) proved to be a good indicator of "how clean is clean?" These and several other Exxon-sponsored studies have shown that the toxicity of oiled sediments declined to clean levels within a few years and hydrocarbon-related toxicity was virtually absent in the shoreline sediments.

Although small amounts of weathered oil remain buried in sediments on a few boulder beaches, the remaining oil is in locations and physical forms that pose no health risk to shoreline biological communities, fish, birds, and mammals. Plant and animal populations that use the shore have recovered from the effects of the oil spill.

CHAPTER 3

Is Oil a Viable Energy Source for the Future?

The World Will Run Out of Oil

Paul Craig Roberts

Paul Craig Roberts, journalist and author of *The End of Oil: On the Edge of a Perilous New World*, contends in this selection that while the world is not going to run out of oil immediately, the future of oil is not promising. He points out that when oil production declines, as it must since it is a finite resource, oil prices will soar, causing economies to crash. The world must learn to move beyond its dependency on oil, Roberts concludes.

The news last month [February 2004] that the vast Saudi oil fields are in decline is a far bigger story than most in the media, or the United States, seem to realize. We may begrudge the Saudis their 30-year stranglehold on the world economy. But even the possibility that the lords of oil have less of the stuff than advertised raises troubling questions. How long will the world's long-term oil supplies last? As important, what will the big importing nations, like the U.S., do the day world oil production hits its inevitable peak?

For more than a century, Western governments have been relentlessly upbeat about the long-term outlook for oil. Whenever pessimists claimed that supplies were running low—as they have many times—oil companies always seemed to discover huge new fields. It's now an article of faith among oil optimists, including those in the U.S. government, that global oil reserves won't run out for at least four decades, which seems like enough time to devise a whole suite of alternative energy technologies to smoothly and seamlessly replace oil.

Paul Craig Roberts, "Running Out of Oil—and Time," *Los Angeles Times*, 2004. Reproduced by permission of Paul Craig Roberts and Creators Syndicate, Inc.

Oil Optimism Is Questionable

But such oil optimism, always questionable, is now more suspect than ever. True, we won't "run out" of oil tomorrow, or even 10 years from now. But the long-term picture is grim. In the first place, it's not a matter of running out of oil but of hitting a production peak. Since 1900, world oil production that—is, the number of barrels we can pump from the ground—has risen in near-perfect step with world oil demand. Today, demand stands at about 29 billion barrels of oil a year, and so does production. By 2020, demand may well be 45 billion barrels a year, by which time, we hope, oil companies will have upped production accordingly.

At some point, however, production simply won't be able to match demand. Oil is an exhaustible resource: The more you produce, the less remains in the ground, and the harder it is to bring up that remainder. We

Though oil reserves are suspected to lie deep under the ocean, they are very difficult and expensive to extract.

won't be "out of oil"; a vast amount will still be flowing—just not quickly enough to satisfy demand. And as any economist can tell you, when supply falls behind demand, bad things happen.

During the 1979 Iranian revolution, the last time oil production fell off significantly, world oil prices hit the modern equivalent of $80 a barrel. And that, keep in mind, was a temporary decline. If world oil production were to truly peak and begin a permanent decline, the effect would be staggering: Prices would not come back down. Any part of the global economy dependent on cheap energy—which is to say, pretty much everything these days—would be changed forever.

Life After the Peak

And that's the good news. The term "peak" tends to suggest a nice, neat curve, with production rising slowly to a halfway point, then tapering off gradually to zero—as if, since it took a century to reach a peak it ought to take another 100 years to reach the end. But in the real world, the landing will not be soft. As we hit the peak, soaring prices—$70, $80, even $100 a barrel—will encourage oil companies and oil states to scour the planet for oil. For a time, they will succeed, finding enough crude to keep production flat, thus stretching out the peak into a kind of plateau and perhaps temporarily easing fears. But in reality, this manic, post-peak production will deplete remaining reserves all the more quickly, thus ensuring that the eventual decline is far steeper and far more sudden. As one U.S. government geologist put it to me recently, "the edge of a plateau looks a lot like a cliff."

As production falls off this cliff, prices won't simply increase; they will fly. If our oil dependence hasn't lessened drastically by then, the global economy is likely to slip into a recession so severe that the Great Depression will look like a dress rehearsal. Oil will cease to be viable as a fuel—hardly an encouraging scenario in a world where oil currently provides 40% of all energy and nearly 90% of all transportation fuel. Political reaction would be desperate. Industrial economies, hungry for energy, would begin making it from any source available—most likely coal—regardless of the ecological consequences. Worse, competition for remaining oil supplies would intensify,

With so much of the world dependent on gas for transportation, an oil shortage could have drastic consequences.

potentially leading to a new kind of political conflict: the energy war.

An Oil Peak Is Near

Thus, when we peak becomes a rather pressing question. Some pessimists tell us the peak has already come, and that calamity is imminent. That's unlikely. But the optimists' forecast—that we don't peak until around 2035—is almost as hard to believe. First, oil demand is climbing faster than optimists had hoped, mainly because China and India, the sleeping giants, are waking up to embrace a Western-style high-energy industrialism that includes tens of millions of new cars. Second, even as oil demand is rising, oil discovery rates are falling. Oil can't be produced without first being found, and the rate at which oil companies are locating new oil fields is in serious decline. The peak for world discoveries was around 1960; today, despite astonishing advances in exploration and production technology, the industry is finding just 12 billion new barrels of oil each year—less than half of what we use. This is one reason that oil prices, which had averaged $20 a barrel since the 1970s, have been hovering at $30 for nearly a year.

Oil companies, not surprisingly, are getting anxious. Despite the fact that the current high oil prices are yielding massive company profits, companies are finding it harder and harder to replace the oil they sell with newly discovered barrels. On average, for every 10 barrels an oil company sells, its exploration teams find just four new barrels—a trend that can go on only so long. Indeed, most Western oil firms now say the only way to halt this slide is to get back into the Middle East, which kicked them out dur-

ANOTHER OPINION

Peak and Final Decline

"World oil production is about to reach a peak and go into its final decline. For years, a handful of petroleum geologists, including me, have been predicting peak oil before 2007, but in an era of cheap oil, few people listened. Lately, several major oil companies seem to have got the message. One of Chevron's ads says the world is currently burning 2 [billion barrels] of oil for every barrel of new oil discovered. ExxonMobil says 1987 was the last year that we found more oil worldwide than we burned. Shell reports that it will expand its Canadian oil-sands operations but elsewhere will focus on finding natural gas and not oil. It sounds as though Shell is kissing the oil business goodbye."

Kenneth Deffeyes, *Time*, October 31, 2005.

ing the OPEC [Organization of the Petroleum Exporting Countries] nationalizations of the 1960s and '70s. This has, in fact, become the mantra of the oil industry: Get us back into the Middle East or be prepared for trouble. And the [George W.] Bush administration seems to have taken the message to heart.

The Middle East Is No Longer the Promised Land

Now, of course, the Middle East is looking less and less like the Promised Land. Western analysts have long feared that the Saudis and other oil-state leaders are too corrupt, unstable and bankrupt to step up their oil production fast enough to meet surging world demand. [Recent] revelations, in which some Saudis themselves expressed doubt over future production increases, have only heightened such concerns.

Put another way, we may not be able to pinpoint exactly when a peak is coming, but recent events suggest that it will be sooner than the optimists have been telling us—perhaps by 2020, or even 2015 if Asian demand picks up as fast as some analysts now expect. What this means is that we can no longer sit back and hope that an alternative to oil will come along in time. Such complacency all but ensures that, when the peak does arrive, our response will be defensive, costly and hugely disruptive. Instead, we must begin now, with every tool at our disposal, to find ways to get "beyond petroleum" if we are to have any hope of controlling the shift from oil to whatever comes next.

2 The World Will Not Run Out of Oil

Julian L. Simon

Julian L. Simon, professor and author of several marketing books, predicts in the following selection that there will be no world oil shortage. Simon views the future optimistically, arguing that in the past humans have always found new sources of energy and will continue to do so in the future. He contends that predictions of oil shortages are illogical, claiming that reserves of energy sources such as oil have always stayed ahead of consumption. Simon asserts that it is misleading to assume that there will be no new developments in oil production that will make oil more available.

Energy is the master resource, because energy enables us to convert one material into another. As natural scientists continue to learn more about the transformation of materials from one form to another with the aid of energy, energy will be even more important. Therefore, if the cost of usable energy is low enough, all other important resources can be made plentiful. . . .

For example, low energy costs would enable people to create enormous quantities of useful land. The cost of energy is the prime reason that water desalination now is too expensive for general use; reduction in energy cost would make water desalination feasible, and irrigated farming would follow in many areas that are now deserts. And if energy were much cheaper, it would be feasible to transport sweet water from areas of surplus to arid

Julian L. Simon, *The Ultimate Resource 2*, Princeton, NJ: Princeton University Press, 1996. © 1996 by Princeton University Press. Reproduced by permission of Princeton University Press.

areas far away. Another example: If energy costs were low enough, all kinds of raw materials could be mined from the sea.

On the other hand, if there were to be an absolute shortage of energy—that is if there were no oil in the tanks, no natural gas in the pipelines, no coal to load onto the railroad cars—then the entire economy would come to a halt. Or if energy were available but only at a very high price, we would produce much smaller amounts of most consumer goods and services.

The question before us is: What is the prospect for oil scarcity and energy prices? . . .

The World Has More Energy, Not Less

The statistical history of energy supplies is a rise in plenty rather than in scarcity. . . . The relevant measures are the production costs of energy as measured in time and money, and the price to the consumer. . . . Suffice it to say that the appropriate interpretation of these data is that they show an unambiguous trend toward lower cost and greater availability of energy.

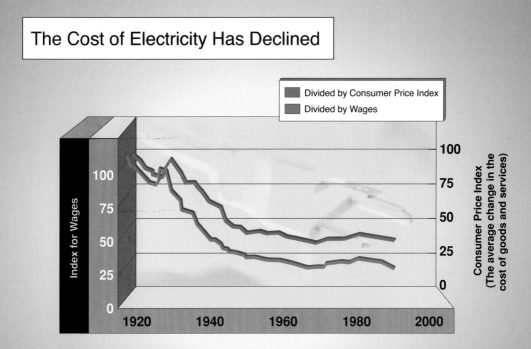

The Cost of Electricity Has Declined

■ Divided by Consumer Price Index
■ Divided by Wages

The price of electricity relative to the consumer price index and wages in the United States

Source: Julian L. Simon, *The Ultimate Resource 2*, 1996

The price of oil fell because of technological advance, of course. The price of a barrel (42 gallons) fell from $4 to thirty-five cents in 1862 because of the innovation of drilling, begun in Pennsylvania in 1859. And the price of a gallon of kerosene fell from fifty-eight cents to twenty-six cents between 1865 and 1870 because of improvements in refining and transportation, many of them by John D. Rockefeller. This meant that the middle class could afford oil lamps at night; earlier, only the rich could afford whale oil and candles, and all others were unable to enjoy the benefits of light.

The price history of *electricity* is particularly revealing because it indicates the price to the consumer, at home or at work. That is, the price of electricity is closer to the price of the *service* we get from energy than are the prices of coal and oil, which are raw materials. . . . The costs of the services matter more than the costs of the raw materials themselves.

The ratio of the price of electricity to the average wage in manufacturing shows that the quantity of electricity bought with an hour's wages has steadily increased. Because each year an hour's work has bought more rather than less electricity, this measure suggests that energy has become ever less troublesome in the economy over the recorded period, no matter what the price of energy in current dollars.

In short, the trends in energy costs and scarcity have been downward over the entire period for which we have data. And such trends are usually the most reliable bases for forecasts. From these data we may conclude with considerable confidence that energy will be less costly and more available in the future than in the past.

The reason that the cost of energy has declined in the long run is the fundamental process of (1) increased demand due to the growth of population and income, which raises prices and hence constitutes opportunity to entrepreneurs and inventors;

(2) the search for new ways of supplying the demand for energy; (3) the eventual discovery of methods which leave us better off than if the original problem had not appeared.

An early illustration of the process: In 300 B.C.E., so much wood was being used for metal smelting that the Roman Senate limited mining. (Using the coercive power of government, instead of the creative power of the market, is a very old idea.) Almost two millennia later, in England, the shortage of wood for use as charcoal in the casting of iron became so acute—it was affecting the building of naval ships—that in 1588 Parliament passed a law against cutting trees for coke in iron making, and then banned the building of new foundries in 1580. Though the use of coal in place of charcoal had been known, there were technical difficulties—impurities that affected the quality of the iron. This time, the wood shortage exerted pressure that led to the development of coal as well as blowing machines to be used in smelting, a keystone in the upcoming Industrial Revolution.

There Will Be No Energy Crisis

You may object that extrapolating a future from past trends of greater and greater abundance is like extrapolating—just before you hit the ground—that a jump from the top of the Eiffel Tower is an exhilarating experience. Please notice, however, that for a jump from the tower we have advance knowledge that there would be a sudden discontinuity when reaching the ground. In the case of energy and natural resources, there is no persuasive advance evidence for a negative discontinuity; rather, the evidence points toward positive discontinuities—nuclear fusion, solar energy, and discoveries of energy sources that we now cannot conceive of. Historical evidence further teaches us that such worries about discontinuities have usually generated the very economic pressures that have opened new frontiers. Hence, there is no solid reason to think that we are about to hit the ground after an energy jump as if from an Eiffel Tower. More likely, we are in a rocket on the ground that has only been warming up until now and will take off sometime soon.

More appropriate than the Eiffel Tower analogy is this joke: Sam falls from a building he is working on, but luckily has hold

Experimental fusion devices like this one in China would be unnecessary if more research concentrated on finding and producing oil.

of a safety rope. Inexplicably he lets go of the rope and hits the ground with a thud. Upon regaining consciousness he is asked: "Why did you let go of the rope?" "Ah," he says, "it was going to break anyway." Analogously, letting go of all the ropes that support the advance of civilization—for example, turning our backs on the best potential sources of energy—is the advice we now receive from energy doomsters and conservationists.

Future Energy Supplies Look Promising

Turning now from trends to theory, we shall consider our energy future in two theoretical contexts: (1) with income and population remaining much as they are now, (2) with different rates of income growth than now. . . . It would be neatest to discuss the United States separately from the world as a whole, but for convenience we shall go back and forth. (The longer the time horizon, the more the discussion refers to the world as a whole rather than just to the United States or the industrialized countries.)

The analysis of energy resembles the analysis of natural resources and food, but energy has special twists that require separate discussion. With these two exceptions, everything said earlier about natural resources applies to energy: (1) On the negative side, energy cannot easily be recycled. (But energy can come much closer to being recycled than one ordinarily thinks. For example, because the fuel supply on warships is very limited, heat from the boilers is passed around water pipes to extract additional calories as it goes up the smokestack.) (2) On the positive side, our energy supplies clearly are not bounded by the Earth. The sun has been the ultimate source of all energy other than nuclear. Therefore, though we cannot recycle energy as we can recycle minerals, our supply of energy is clearly not limited by the Earth's present contents, and hence it is not "finite" in any sense at all—not even in the nonoperational sense.

Furthermore, humanity burned wood for thousands of years before arriving at coal, burned coal about three hundred years before developing oil, and burned oil about seventy years before inventing nuclear fission. Is it reasonable and prudent to assume that sometime in the next seven billion years—or even

Fusion energy will ultimately be replaced by other sources of energy.

seven hundred or seventy years—humanity will not arrive at a cheaper and cleaner and more environmentally benign substitute for fission energy?

But let us turn to a horizon relevant for social decisions—the next five, twenty-five, one hundred, perhaps two hundred years. And let us confine ourselves to the practical question of what is likely to happen to the cost of energy relative to other goods, and in proportion to our total output.

The Law of Diminishing Returns Is a Myth

First let us dispose of the "law of diminishing returns" with respect to energy. Here is how Barry Commoner uses this idea:

> [T]he law of diminishing returns [is] the major reason why the United States has turned to foreign sources for most of its oil. Each barrel [of oil] drawn from the earth causes the next one to be more difficult to obtain. The economic consequence is that it causes the cost to increase continuously.

[In a 1975 letter to the editor of the *New York Times*,] another environmentalist explains her version of the "law of diminishing returns" with respect to oil:

> We must now extract our raw materials from ever more degraded and inaccessible deposits. This means that ever more of our society's precious investment capital must be diverted to this process and less is available for consumption and real growth. Fifty years ago, getting oil required little more than sticking a pipe in the ground. Now we must invest several billion dollars to open up the Alaska oilfields to deliver the same product. *Economists, if they stood this process as well as physical scientists*, might call it the declining productivity of capital [law of diminishing returns].

All these quotes are just plain wrong; it costs less today to get oil from the ground in prime sources than it cost fifty years ago to get it from the ground in prime sources. . . .

In brief, there is no compelling theoretical reason why we should eventually run out of energy, or even why energy should be more scarce and costly in the future than it is now.

America Should Transition from Oil to Renewable Energy

Stephen Leeb and Donna Leeb

In the following article, Stephen Leeb and Donna Leeb contend that rising oil prices caused by diminishing reserves will make renewable energy sources economically competitive. The authors assert that the U.S. government must create a comprehensive plan to replace dirty fossil fuels such as oil with clean energy sources such as wind. Such a transition will benefit the environment and reduce America's dependence on foreign oil. Stephen Leeb is a financial adviser. Together, Stephen Leeb and Donna Leeb have published several books on the U.S. economy and investing.

Arthur C. Clarke is best known as a science fiction writer, in particular as the author of *2001: A Space Odyssey*. He also, however, is a well-respected scientist and philosopher who was knighted for a variety of achievements, among them the invention of the communications satellite. Now in his eighties, he has been living for some time in Sri Lanka. In the fall of 1999 the science section of the *New York Times* carried a fascinating interview with Clarke about his thoughts on the future of the universe and the human race. That interview was the catalyst for this book.

Real Problems Facing the World

One question put to Clarke was how he felt about the recent announcement that the world's population had reached six billion. He replied: "Well, I feel rather depressed, but then there are so many times when I'm an optimist. I think we have a 51 percent chance of survival. I would say the next decade is perhaps one of the most crucial in human history, though many people have felt that way in the past. But it's real now. There are so many things coming to a head simultaneously. The population. The environment. The energy crunch. And, of course, the dangers of nuclear warfare. I am often asked to predict things, and I'm described as a prophet, but I deny that. I'm just an extrapolator. I can envision a whole spectrum of futures, very few of which are desirable."

Those words resonated with us. And as we thought about them, it seemed that of the four issues he singled out—the population explosion, the environment, energy, and nuclear warfare—in many ways energy was the most important, because it could be the key to solving the rest. With respect to population growth, if we could develop clean, renewable energies, we'd be able to desalinate the ocean and provide adequate food and water for growing populations. Moreover, as nations become

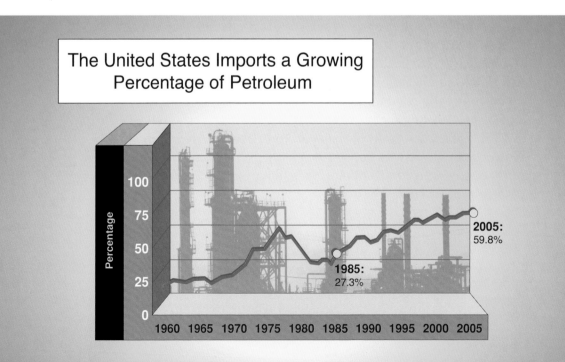

The United States Imports a Growing Percentage of Petroleum

2005: 59.8%

1985: 27.3%

Source: *Annual Energy Review*, 2003. U.S. Department of Energy

more economically developed, a process that cheap energy would foster, population growth invariably slows down. Finally, once energy became abundant and cheap, our space program would have no limits. Colonizing other worlds, which doubtless seems very far-fetched and remote today, could happen—but if and only if we develop cheap and abundant energy.

As far as the environment goes, if we stopped burning coal and oil, we'd instantly end the major source of environmental degradation. And a world with limitless energy is also a world far less threatened by nuclear warfare, for several reasons. First, poverty would diminish, and there'd be far less reason for poorer nations or people to seek to take up arms against wealthier nations. Also, once we're no longer economically hostage to unstable and hostile oil-producing nations in the Middle East and elsewhere, we'll be far more able to root out any terrorism that remains in those areas. Finally, it would become feasible to dismantle all nuclear plants, eliminating any further production of weapons-grade plutonium. . . .

Rising Oil Prices Will Force Change

One problem [with developing energy alternatives] has been that for a long time the whole issue of alternative energies has been seen largely in the context of an overall political gestalt. If you're the kind of person who cares about alternative energies, you probably also are a vegetarian or at the very least are into organic foods, and chances are you're some kind of artist or maybe a teacher or social worker. If you're made of tougher stuff, a construction worker or a corporate executive, you know that it's oil that makes the world go round.

This dichotomy was perhaps best symbolized by the actions of two presidents. Jimmy Carter, he of the professorial-like cardigan sweaters, installed solar panels in the White House. Ronald Reagan, the cowboy president, ripped them out.

Today, however, the issue of energy alternatives is catching up with us. We're running out of time, and as oil production peaks, we no longer will have the luxury of treating alternative fuels as a matter of politics or style or as something we can leave for a later generation. Instead, it will become a central issue for us all. To put it even more strongly, the survival of our capitalist

Former U.S. presidents Ronald Reagan (left) and Jimmy Carter disagreed over whether alternative energy sources such as solar power could offer America energy independence.

system will depend on our ability to resolve it. If that seems too extreme a statement, it's not. Our system can't survive without affordable energy, and once oil doesn't fit that bill, we'll need to find something else that does. We'll all have to come together on this.

Rising oil prices will force the issue. But even then we can't take for granted that we will get on the right path. We can't rely on good old-fashioned capitalism and the profit motive to produce solutions, to generate the best technology or create the necessary infrastructure. Private enterprise will play a big role, but it can't do it all on its own.

America's signal accomplishments during the twentieth century—whether winning wars, building the interstate highway system, or landing a man on the moon—required efforts well beyond the reach of private enterprise. They required intense and massive cooperation between the private and public sectors. Developing alternative energies will be no different.

This will be an enormous challenge and also an immense opportunity. Just as the space program and the highway program created many new industries in this country and helped promote economic growth, so will the development of alternative energies. And whether we like to admit it or not, this is a country in dire need of new industries. As an ever greater portion of our manufacturing base has been transferred to low-labor-cost countries such as China, our leadership rests almost entirely on our

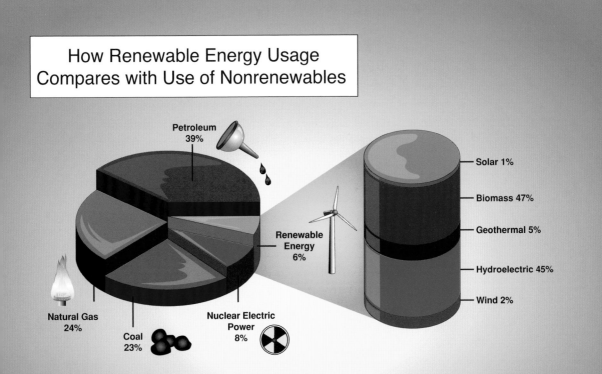

How Renewable Energy Usage Compares with Use of Nonrenewables

Petroleum 39%

Natural Gas 24%

Coal 23%

Nuclear Electric Power 8%

Renewable Energy 6%

Solar 1%

Biomass 47%

Geothermal 5%

Hydroelectric 45%

Wind 2%

Source: U.S. Department of Energy, 2002. www.eia.doe.gov

superiority in defense. Is this a large enough peg? Maybe over the short term. But without energy, even the strongest defense apparatus will grind to a halt.

If the U.S. can establish a leadership position in the development of alternative energies, we'll not only have successfully met the tremendous challenge of declining oil supplies. We'll have built a vital new industry based on vital new technologies that will spur economic growth and ensure our continued hegemony in the world community.

A Full-Fledged Commitment Is Required

What's required? Making a full-fledged commitment to wind energy by helping to fund a nationwide network of turbines, while funding long-range research into improved solar cell technology and hydrogen storage. Having a clear goal, as we did in putting a man on the moon. And launching this effort now. It's already late in the day. The sooner we make a real commitment, the better, because there will be no deus ex machina [a God in the Machine] to bail us out. Token funding of alternative energies won't be enough. Our whole national mindset has to change.

It would have been nice, of course, if the big push to develop alternative energies had been made before we reached this pass. Even before the first Arab oil embargo it was clear to some people that it made no sense to rely so heavily on fossil fuels. Buckminster Fuller was an early visionary in this area, as in many others. In 1969 he wrote in his book *Utopia or Oblivion*: "There are gargantuan energy-income sources available which do not stay the processes of nature's own conservation of energy within the earth's crust 'against a rainy day.' These are in water, tidal, wind, and desert-impinging sun radiation power. The exploiters of fossil fuels, coal and oil, say it costs less to produce and burn the savings account. This is analogous to saying it takes less effort to rob a bank than to do the work which the money deposited in the bank represents. The question is cost to whom? To our great-great-grandchildren, who will have no fossil fuels to turn the machines? I find that the ignorant acceptance by world society's presently deputized leaders of the momentarily expedient and the lack of constructive, long-distance thinking

Wind farms
currently supply
America with just
two percent of its
energy needs.

—let alone comprehensive thinking— . . . render dubious the case for humanity's earthian future."

There are many reasons for our failure to move ahead on the alternative energy front sooner. The factors, for sure, would include the intricate realities of Middle East politics and diplomacy and the clout of oil companies. But in the final analysis it likely comes down to the inherent shortsightedness of the human race, our disinclination to endure immediate pain in the hope of long-term gain. . . .

For a long time, the simple fact was that oil and other fossil fuels were a lot cheaper than any prospective alternatives. For alternative fuels to have made it onto the playing field, the government would have had to step in and take action, such as steeply raising the price of oil through taxes. One way or another, such steps would have made life tremendously more expensive for the entire voting public, not an intrinsically appealing idea to your typical politician. Even if, say, an enlightened president was interested in doing this, getting a majority of Congress to go along would not have been a good bet. . . .

[However,] as oil prices continue to go higher, the need to move beyond oil will finally get everyone's full attention. There have been oil scares in the recent past. But as we hope we've shown, this one will be different—this one isn't just going to go away. As Clarke said in the passage quoted above, this time it's real. We are facing a momentous transition, one that requires real leadership and massive effort and funding. This transitional period will be marked by both turbulence and opportunity. Most important, unless we truly blow things, it ultimately should result in a far better world, one where growth is based on renewable, nonpolluting energies that can create happier lives for everyone on this planet. That truly will be a revolution worth participating in.

A Transition to Renewable Energy Is Impractical

Peter W. Huber and Mark P. Mills

In the following excerpt from their book *The Bottomless Well*,
Peter W. Huber and Mark P. Mills argue that alternative energy sources are inefficient, impractical, and harmful to the
environment. Contrary to popular belief, using organic matter such as corn for fuel is worse for the environment than
using oil because of the enormous amounts of land required
to grow the crops. Additionally, they claim, solar and wind
power cannot produce the amounts of energy needed to fuel
modern economies. Huber is a senior fellow at the Manhat-
tan Institute's Center for Legal Policy, specializing in issues
in science and technology. Mills is a physicist and a founder
of Digital Power Capital, a company focusing on new technologies that create more efficient power.

W hat would it take to reverse course and return today's
America to a carbohydrate-fueled economy? Some people propose just that—solar energy that's literally green. "Till-
ing, not drilling," they advocate. "Biology, not geology. Living
carbon, not dead carbon. Vegetables, not minerals." A great
shift back, in short, to what a group called the Institute for
Local Self-Reliance extols as the "carbohydrate economy."
Which is to say: agriculture. Suitably enhanced, perhaps, to
raise yields. "We need to go from black gold to green gold," de-

clares the director of biotechnology development at DuPont. Farmers certainly love the idea, and their votes have produced decades of federal subsidies for corn-based ethanol fuel.

Oil Is an Efficient Energy Source

Yet however preposterous the idea may sound, drilling for oil and building an SUV-grade highway system uses 10 times *less* land, per mile and per useful pound moved, than growing food to fuel a bicyclist. The SUV starts out 300 times worse than the bike—because it moves 30 times the weight of its driver in steel, and because it needs 10 times more roadway per useful pound moved. In terms of land surface occupied to extract and deliver the energy used, however, crude oil is at least 1,000 times more

The alternative fuel ethanol is produced from corn. Though ethanol burns clean, growing the required amount of corn could devastate American farmland.

frugal than grain. And a car engine, and the refining and distribution systems behind it, are about twice as efficient in converting crude oil to locomotion than the grain-bread-muscle systems that stand between plants and the pedals on a bike; make that 16 times as efficient if the biker favors meat.

Or to turn the numbers around, 2 acres of top-notch timber-growing forest can yield a sustainable 40 tons per year of wood biomass, from which you can extract the liquid fuel equivalent of 130 gallons of gasoline, which will then propel an average car about 3,000 miles. Today, by comparison, the average American uses about 2 acres of land for *all* dwelling, roads, farm, range, and energy—the whole lot. Plowing for carbohydrates adds more carbon to the air than mining for coal or drilling for oil, because the solar-carbohydrate refineries—farms—require such huge amounts of cleared land. Which means that the carbohydrate-fueled stomach is a whole lot worse for the atmosphere than the hydro-carbon-fueled motor that has replaced it.

However unlikely the numbers may sound, they are easy to verify. They are, indeed, almost obvious once one gets used to seeing plants, cows, horses, and bikers for what they are: land-hungry, territory-expanding automatons, optimized for survival and reproduction, not for supplying power to others. To be sure, a bike or a horse *looks* incomparably greener than an SUV or eighteen-wheel truck, but only because we think of cornfield and pasture as "natural."

People everywhere grasp that energy is the key to survival and prosperity, and until they can satisfy their insatiable demand for energy in other ways, they satisfy it by occupying more land. Only very recently, and only in a few countries, have people discovered how to sever the link between wealth and land. Land-poor Europe leveled most of its forests centuries ago and is now preoccupied with protecting the cow pastures of reactionary farmers. Much of the developing world still depends largely on agriculture. But—thanks to fossil fuels—North America has reversed direction.

Solar Energy Is Inadequate

Growing grass in a pasture isn't the only way to transform solar energy into horsepower. For efficient, reliable, round-the-clock

The Hoover Dam is an environmental catch-22: It runs on clean solar energy but its creation damaged the environment.

capture of solar energy, no other technology yet comes close to the one incorporated in the Hoover Dam, which counts on the sun to lift the water that spins its turbines. But like ethanol farms, dams may cost you a forest or two, upstream.

Selenium-doped silicon wafers mounted in glass or plastic can currently capture about 30 watts per square meter [W/m^2] on a round-the-clock average in the United States—making photovoltaics (PV) about forty times better than the typical leaf of a green plant, and over ten times better than an intensively cultivated cornfield. But New York consumes 55 W/m^2 of energy. So to power New York with PV, you would have to cover every square inch of the city's horizontal surface with wafers—and then extend the PV sprawl over at least twice that area again. A Pentium 4 microprocessor consumes about 20 watts per square *centimeter*—which is to say, ten thousand times more, in power density terms, than a PV solar cell can generate—and semiconductor-grade silicon for digital circuits is currently being shipped ten times faster than silicon for PV cells.

Doubling the Human Footprint

The fuels we rely on currently, by contrast, are well matched to the modern city's intensely concentrated demand for power. A coal mine yields something like 5,000 W/m^2 of land, an oil field double that, and a uranium mine, together with enrichment facilities, at least a hundred times more. Environmentally speaking, conventional fuels get steadily worse from there on out —for every acre used in extracting them, we use another 2 acres or so for track, pipeline, and power line to transport or transmit. But refineries are needed to transform corn into ethanol, too, and generating any significant share of our electricity with PV cells would require more grid, not less, because large solar arrays must sprawl over such wide areas. Rooftops do offer some spare real estate for solar capture, but nowhere near enough. Desert sands and rocky plateaus offer some additional ecologically dead surface but usually at great distances from where people live—which means using up more (and better) land hauling the energy back to the people.

Despite decades of subsidy and government promotion, "renewables" (other than conventional hydro) now generate

Critics of solar power complain that the installation of solar panels on vast swaths of land poses threats to prairie wildlife.

barely 0.7 percent of our electricity. Regulators have forced electric utilities to buy renewables—at an average price about three times higher than they pay for conventional sources of supply. Add in the forest industry's on-site burning of waste wood, and renewables contribute perhaps 3 percent of all the energy we consume.

No conceivable mix of solar, biomass, or wind technology could meet even half our current energy demand without (at the very least) doubling the human footprint on the surface of the continent. Humanity burns 345 Quads [quadrillion Btu's] of fossil fuel energy per year and a good bit more wood and dung on top of that. All the plants on the surface of the planet capture only an estimated 2,000 Quads of energy through photosynthesis, and that energy is already being used—to grow wilderness.

Facts About Oil

Properties of Oil

- Oil comes from plants and animals that lived in the seas millions of years ago. When these plants and animals died, their bodies sank to the seabed and became buried and compressed. Under increasing pressure, they formed oil.
- When oil is first taken from the earth, it is called crude oil and is later often referred to simply as oil. Oil can flow like water or can be thick. Oil can be yellow, red, green, brown, or black.

Historical Uses of Oil

- Ancient Egyptians used oil to preserve their mummies.
- The Chinese used oil for heating, cooking, and making bricks.
- Native Americans used oil for heating, lighting, and making medicines.

Modern Uses of Oil

- Fuel
- Plastics
- Detergents
- Paints
- Clothing made from nylon and polyester
- Insulation
- Synthetic rubber for items such as shoes and tires

Oil Statistics

- Oil has been used for over eight thousand years.
- Oil has been discovered on every continent except Antarctica.

- More than half of the world's oil is in the Middle East.
- Edwin L. Drake built the first modern oil well in Pennsylvania in 1859.
- The main offshore oilfields are beneath the Persian Gulf, the Gulf of Mexico, and in the North Sea between Scotland and Norway.
- The world's largest oil refinery is in Ras Tanura, Saudi Arabia. It is owned by Saudi Aramco.
- Oil accounts for nearly 31 percent of the world's fuel consumption.
- The United States consumes nearly 25 percent of the world's total oil consumption.
- U. S. oil consumption was 17 million barrels per day in 1990. In 2004 it was up to nearly 20 million barrels per day.
- In the last twenty-five years, the number of oil refineries in the United States fell to 149, less than half the number in 1981.
- In the last twenty-five years, gas consumption has risen 45 percent.
- Fuel economy for U.S. automobiles was lower in 2002 than at any time since 1981.
- The price of oil per barrel hit a record high of over $70 per barrel in April 2006.

Costs of Oil per Barrel

1995	under $20 per barrel
1996	under $20 per barrel
1997	$25 per barrel
1998	under $20 per barrel
1999	$12–$13 per barrel
2000	$30 per barrel
2001	under $30 per barrel
2002	$20 per barrel

2003	$30 per barrel
2004	$30–$35 per barrel
2005	$45–$55 per barrel
2006	(April) over $70 per barrel

Methods of Drilling for Oil

- Oil is extracted from the earth by drilling down through the earth's crust. A drill bit is attached to a pipe and rotated so that it cuts a hole through the rock. When a drill finally reaches oil, the pipe attached to it can be up to a mile long or even more. Since oil is often trapped underground at very high pressures, when the drill reaches the oil, the oil can rush to the earth's surface. When this happens, the oil wells are called "gushers," but gushers are not very common today because new technology provides for special valves at the wellhead to control flow.

- At the turn of the twenty-first century, about one-third of the world's oil came from beneath the ocean. Offshore oil rigs are platforms that are built to stand on the seabed or even float on the ocean. A floating platform can work at depths of 3,300 feet (1,000 meters). For the deepest waters, there are drill ships that can work at depths of 8,000 feet (2,400 meters).

Oil Infrastructure

- After oil has been taken from the ground, it is called crude oil. Oil is not useful in this form and therefore must be processed. Oil refineries process the oil and prepare it for a variety of uses. There are fewer than 150 refineries in the United States, a number that is decreasing compared to the recent past. Oil is made up of many liquids, including gasoline and kerosene. When the oil is heated at refineries, these liquids can be separated. There are two main ways to refine oil: distillation and cracking. Both methods use heat to separate the ingredients of oil, but cracking adds chemical processes to increase the amount of gasoline produced. After the ingredients are separated, pipelines, trucks, and ships (called oil tankers) deliver the refined oil to other factories all over the world for a variety of uses. The largest oil tankers carry more than four hundred thousand tons of oil at a time. The largest oil pipeline in the world is in Canada; it carries oil 2,353 miles (3,787 kilometers) from Edmonton, Alberta, to Montreal, Quebec.

Glossary

barrel (bbl.): A measurement used in the oil industry for a unit of volume of oil or oil products equivalent to 158.978 liters or 42 U.S. gallons.

bitumen: Another term for hydrocarbons. Petroleum is sometimes referred to as bituminous.

carbon dioxide: A gas composed of one carbon and two oxygen atoms, often referred to as CO_2. Carbon dioxide gas is released when fossil fuels such as oil are burned. It acts as a greenhouse gas, trapping the sun's heat and warming the earth.

cracking: Processes using heat and chemical reactions to help break down crude oil for conversion into more useful materials.

crude oil: A mineral oil consisting of a mixture of hydrocarbons of natural origin, yellow to black in color, of variable specific gravity and viscosity.

derrick: Tower holding the drilling machinery that stands over an oil well.

distillation: The first stage in the refining process in which crude oil is heated and unfinished petroleum products are initially separated.

fossil fuels: Fuels having a high carbon and hydrogen content that are made up of the remains of organisms preserved in rocks in the earth's crust. Oil and coal are examples of fossil fuels.

fuel oil: Oil that is heavily distilled in the refining process. This type of oil is frequently used for supplying energy to power stations and factories.

gas oil: A moderately distilled oil, which is often used for diesel fuel.

greenhouse effect: The process by which gases in the atmosphere trap the sun's heat and warm the planet. The major greenhouse gases are water vapor, carbon dioxide, and ozone.

hydrocarbons: Compounds containing only hydrogen and carbon atoms. These compounds may be in solid, liquid, or gaseous form.

natural gas: Petroleum in gaseous form consisting of light hydrocarbons. Methane is the most dominant component of natural gas.

oil rig: Offshore platform used for drilling for oil.

petrochemicals: Chemicals such as ethylene, propylene, and benzene that are derived from petroleum.

petroleum: Very broad term referring to all liquid hydrocarbons which can be collected from the earth.

refining: The process of using heat, pressure, and chemicals to convert crude oil into usable fuel products such as gasoline, kerosene, diesel oil, and lubricating oil.

reserves: An economically recoverable quantity of crude oil or gas.

Chronology

2000 B.C.
The Chinese refine oil to use for lighting and heat.

A.D. 600–700
Arab and Persian chemists use oil to create "Greek fire," a substance similar to napalm.

1750
A French military officer notes that the Native Americans near present-day Pittsburgh ceremonially set fire to an oil slick in a creek.

1859
Edwin L. Drake taps the first oil well near Titusville, Pennsylvania. Crude oil soon replaces whale oil as the most common choice for lighting.

1870
John D. Rockefeller establishes the Standard Oil Company. Rockefeller's monopoly and tactics establish a business model still referred to as "Big Oil."

1876
Nikolaus Otto builds the first practical gasoline-powered engine.

1890s
Mass production of the automobile begins.

1904
Ida Tarbell publishes *The History of the Standard Oil Company*, a book exposing the corrupt business practices of Rockefeller's Standard Oil.

1914–1918
World War I takes place. The world learns the benefit of oil-fueled machines in times of war.

1920

There are 9 million automobiles in the United States. The oil industry responds by opening gas stations all over the country in the decade ahead.

1944

Near the end of World War II, U.S. president Franklin Roosevelt and British prime minister Winston Churchill tap Middle Eastern oil reserves.

1950

Oil becomes the most used energy source because of automobiles. Oil today remains the world's most used energy source.

1966

The Organization of the Petroleum Exporting Countries (OPEC) is formed by countries to protect their oil resources.

1973

The Arab oil embargo takes place. Some OPEC countries stop selling oil to the United States. Some gas stations run out of gas.

1980

Oil prices continue to increase. The OPEC embargo prompts the Carter Doctrine. The Carter Doctrine makes it the official U.S. policy to use "any means necessary" to protect oil in the Middle East.

1981

The United States responds to the 1978–1980 oil crisis by removing price controls for oil. For the first time since the early 1970s, market forces set the price of oil.

1986

When OPEC stops limiting oil production, the market is flooded. Oil prices collapse.

1991

The Persian Gulf War provides the first significant test of the Carter Doctrine when U.S. troops force Iraq out of Kuwait.

1993

The United States for the first time imports more oil and refined products than it produces. This trend continues.

1998

The large recessions of the Asian economies lead to a decrease in the world demand for oil. Oil prices plummet.

2001

U.S. oil production is 41 percent lower than the 1972 peak. Oil consumption in the United States reaches an all-time high of nearly 20 million barrels per day.

2003

The United States invades Iraq. While the Bush administration first claims that the war was needed to rid Iraq of weapons of mass destruction and end that nation's support for terrorists, the administration later contends that the war was intended to free the Iraqi people from Saddam Hussein's dictatorship and bring democracy to the region. Critics, however, argue that the war in Iraq was waged to secure the nation's huge oil reserves.

2006

In his January State of the Union address, President George W. Bush declares that the United States is "addicted to oil" and calls for research into alternative fuels. In April the price of oil per barrel is over $70 per barrel, an all-time high.

For Further Reading

Books and Papers

Nathan Aaseng, *Business Builders in Oil*. Minneapolis: Oliver, 2000.

Jill Crystal, *Oil and Politics in the Gulf: Rulers and Merchants in Kuwait and Qatar*. New York: Cambridge University Press, 1900.

Art Davidson, *In the Wake of the Exxon Valdez: The Devastating Impact of the Alaskan Oil Spill*. San Francisco: Sierra Club Books, 1990.

Kenneth S. Deffeyes, *Beyond Oil: The View from Hubbert's Peak*. New York: Farrar, Straus, and Giroux, 2005.

Christin Ditchfield, *Oil*. New York: Children's Press, 2002.

Lesley A. DuTemple, *Oil Spills*. San Diego, CA: Lucent, 1999.

Helen Frost, ed., *Season of Dead Water*. Portland, OR: Breitenbush, 1990.

Ian Graham, *Fossil Fuels*. Austin, TX: Raintree Steck-Vaughn, 1999.

Michael T. Klare, *Blood and Oil: The Dangers and Consequences of America's Growing Dependency on Imported Petroleum*. New York: Henry Holt, 2005.

Lutz Kleveman, *The New Great Game: Blood and Oil in Central Asia*. New York: Atlantic Monthly Press, 2003.

Steve Parker, *Oil and Gas*. Milwaukee: Gareth Stevens, 2004.

Matthew R. Simmons, *Twilight in the Desert: The Coming Saudi Oil Shock and the World Economy*. Hoboken, NJ: John Wiley and Sons, 2005.

Page Spencer, *White Silk and Black Tar: A Journal of the Alaska Oil Spill*. Minneapolis: Bergamot, 1990.

Matthew Yeomans, *Oil: Anatomy of an Industry*. New York: New Press, 2004.

Periodicals

Ronald Bailey, "Peak Oil Panic," *Reason*, May 2006.

Christian Science Monitor, "Creeping Toward Oil as a Social Good," April 26, 2006.

Brian Doherty, "Crude Economics," *Reason*, May 2006.

James Terry Duce, "The Changing Oil Industry," *Foreign Affairs*, July 1962.

Economist, "A Hungry Dragon," October 2, 2004.

Esquire, "The History," October 2005.

Daniel Glick, "The Big Thaw," *National Geographic*, September 2004.

Scott Johnson, Michael Hastings, and Christopher Dickey, "Baghdad's Big Oil Bust," *Newsweek*, January 30, 2006.

Brad Knickerbocker, "The Big Spill," *Christian Science Monitor*, March 22, 1999.

Marianne Lavelle, "The New Oil Rush," *U.S. News & World Report*, April 24, 2006.

Mark Levine, "Waist Deep in Big Oil," *Nation*, December 12, 2005.

Doug Moss, "The Spoils of Oil," *E: The Environmental Magazine*, January/February 2006.

National Geographic, "Oil: Where Is It and How Much Is Left?" June 2004.

Paul Phillips, "The American Empire Meets Peak Oil," *Canadian Dimension*, January/February 2006.

John Pullin, "The End of Oil?" *Automotive Engineer*, February 2006.

Jane Bryant Quinn, Temma Ehrenfeld, and Ramin Setoodeh, "The Price of Our Addiction," *Newsweek*, April 24, 2006.

Alex Scott and Michelle Bryner, "Alternative Fuels," *Chemical Week*, November 23, 2005.

USA Today, "Big Oil Pumps Profits at Consumers' Expense," April 26, 2006.

USA Today, "39 Million Reasons Why $3 Gas May Change America," April 27, 2006.

Web Sites

American Petroleum Institute, http://api-ec.api.org. The API is an organization representing America's oil and natural gas industries. This site provides links to information on how gasoline is made and how much oil is left in the world. The site also offers a link to information on what products are developed from a barrel of oil.

The Association for the Study of Peak Oil, www.mbendi.com. The ASPO is a worldwide organization offering information to the public about what it sees as an impending world oil and energy crisis. The site offers links to purchasable material but also provides free links to information on the oil and gas industry.

Energy Information Administration, www.eia.doe.gov. The Energy Information Administration is an organization providing official energy statistics. The site offers links to information about a variety of energy sources, including oil. The site offers games, history, and energy facts, as well.

Organization of the Petroleum Exporting Countries (OPEC), www.opec.org. This official Web site of OPEC offers information on the organization as well as oil itself. It includes links to information on OPEC oil reserves and uses for oil.

Paleontological Research Institution (PRI), www.priweb.org. PRI offers a visual and user-friendly Web site addressing the common uses of oil, history of oil by major discoveries, geology basics, and information on the tools used to find oil in the earth.

United States Environmental Protection Agency, www.epa.gov. This site offers information on how the U.S. government responds to all kinds of oil spills. The "Learning Center" link connects readers to basic information on different types of oil spills and how these spills are cleaned up.

Wayne Pafko Web Site, www.pafko.com. Wayne Pafko, a chemical engineer, is the author of this site, which is designed to offer information on the history of oil, modern refining, and distillation. His site also offers a list of terms important in the oil industry.

Index

Picture Credits

Cover: © Royalty-Free/CORBIS
AFP/Getty Images, 85
© Andrea Merola/epa/CORBIS, 49
AP/Wide World Photos, 64, 75, 78, 83, 115
© Bettmann/CORBIS, 17, 23, 27, 29, 32, 34
© Bin Sheng/epa/CORBIS, 102
© Bob Sacha/CORBIS, 58
© Chuck Eckert/Alamy, 72
Dirck Halstead/Time Life Pictures/Getty Images, 108 (main)
Dr. Robert Muntefering/Getty Images, 12
Eastcott Momatiuk/The Image Bank/Getty Images, 89
© Everett Kennedy Brown/epa/CORBIS, 103
Getty Images, 15
Jagadeesh Nv/Landov, 95
JEROME DELAY/AFP/Getty Images, 108 (inset)
© Jerry and Marcy Monkman/EcoPhotography/Alamy, 63
Keith Wood/Getty Images, 91
© Leonard de Selva/CORBIS, 21
© Norman Godwin/CORBIS, 55
© Peter Roggenthin/dpa/CORBIS, 119
Photos.com, 77 (both), 93 (both), 111, 117
Reportage/Getty Images, 11
© Reuters/CORBIS, 88
Steve Zmina, 22, 37, 41, 43, 45, 52, 66, 70, 84, 99, 106, 109
Steven J. Kazlowski/Alamy 69
Terje Rakke/Getty Images, 57
© Terry Fincher.Photo Int/Alamy, 81
VEER Dale O'Dell/Photonica/Getty Images, 47

About the Editor

Crystal McCage holds a PhD in Rhetoric and Composition and teaches Composition and Children's Literature at a small college in Oregon. She has written several nonfiction books and many reference articles. This is her first book for Greenhaven Press.